SURPRISED
by Healing

"ONE OF THE
GREATEST HEALING MIRACLES
OF THE 20TH CENTURY"
—SID ROTH

DELORES WINDER WITH **BILL KEITH**

DESTINY IMAGE® PUBLISHERS, INC.
P.O. Box 310, Shippensburg, PA 17257-0310

"Speaking to the Purposes of God for This Generation and for the Generations to Come."

This book and all other Destiny Image, Revival Press, MercyPlace, Fresh Bread, Destiny Image Fiction, and Treasure House books are available at Christian bookstores and distributors worldwide.

For a U.S. bookstore nearest you, call 1-800-722-6774.
For more information on foreign distributors, call 717-532-3040.
Or reach us on the Internet: www.destinyimage.com

ISBN 10: 0-7684-3115-8   ISBN 13: 978-0-7684-3115-5

Previously published as: *Joy Comes in the Morning: One of the Greatest Healing Miracles of the 20th Century*

Previously published ISBN #0-910267-04-9

For Worldwide Distribution, Printed in the U.S.A.

1 2 3 4 5 6 7 8 9 10 11 / 13 12 11 10 09

DEDICATION

If Dr. Richard Owellen had not obeyed the Lord's prompting to come to Dallas, Texas, that Saturday, I would not be here today. *"My people are destroyed from lack of knowledge"* (Hos. 4:6). I had no knowledge of healing for today. The word of knowledge for my healing came to him. I am grateful for his obedience. Dr. Owellen is now with the Lord.

CONTENTS

FOREWORD
BY CAROL GRAY

*"Not by might nor by power,
but by My Spirit," says the Lord Almighty*
(Zechariah 4:6).

It was on August 30, 1975, when Delores Winder attended a Methodist conference on the Holy Spirit in Dallas, Texas, where Kathryn Kuhlman was speaking, that the above Scripture became a reality in her life. Facing death, terminally ill with pseudoarthrosis, and having been in a body cast for over 14 years, Delores was only seeking to receive something from God that she could leave with her young son Chris when she died. She received the answer that night in Dallas, as she felt the very presence of the living God surrounding her.

Never having seen a miraculous healing take place and believing that supernatural healing ended with the apostles, Delores was not praying for a physical miracle. However, we have a God who *"is able to do exceeding abundantly above all that we ask or think"* (Eph. 3:20 KJV), and she was transformed from hopelessness to wholeness, totally set free from the disease that had her bound.

So marvelous was Delores's healing, she appeared on Kathryn Kuhlman's television program, *I Believe in Miracles,* and her medically documented healing was included in the book *Real Miracles* by H. Richard

Casdorph, M.D., Ph.D. (See Appendix.) And as you read Delores's own thrilling account in the pages that follow, you too will have the assurance that with God no illness or situation is hopeless.

God has a perfect plan for each life. Having surrendered their lives to God's will, Bill and Delores formed Fellowship Foundation, Inc. and they have been used mightily in a salvation and healing ministry that has reached across this country and into other nations as well.

God is no respecter of persons, and what He did for Delores, He will do for you. Always remember, joy comes in the morning; for regardless of any need you may be facing, God is with you, and there is nothing impossible with Him!

Carol Gray
The Kathryn Kuhlman Foundation

INTRODUCTION
BY SID ROTH

RISE AND WALK

I have passionately investigated miracles for over 30 years. Without a doubt, Delores Winder received one of the greatest verified healing miracles of the 20th century. Miracles like this were *normal* when Jesus walked the earth. Sadly, today it is anything but the norm. This is about to change.

God is raising up a new generation like John the Baptist, who walked *"in the spirit and power of Elijah"* (Luke 1:17). Just *"before the coming of the great and dreadful day of the Lord"* (Mal. 4:5 NKJV), Elijah will arise *"to make ready a people prepared for the Lord"* (Luke 1:17). This Elijah generation will *"turn the hearts of the fathers to their children, and the hearts of the children to their fathers..."* (Mal. 4:6).

Paul calls the Jewish people the *"fathers"* (Rom. 9:5 NKJV). If the fathers represent the Jewish people, then it is obvious who the children are. They are the Christians.

I believe the Elijah generation will be birthed when Jew and Gentile come together in Messiah Jesus as the "One New Man" (see Eph. 2:14-15). When the ancient Jewish spiritual DNA merges with the New Covenant Gentile spiritual DNA, miracles will increase in order to reach the Jew with the Good News. First Corinthians 1:22 says, *"For the Jews require a sign"* (KJV).

We are at the fullness of the Gentile Age. Paul says in Romans 11:25 that *"blindness in part has happened to Israel until the fullness of the Gentiles has come in"* (NKJV). And what happens at the fullness of the Gentile Age? *"All Israel will be saved"* (Rom. 11:26). How will all Israel be saved? According to Paul, it will be when the Gentile Christians provoke the Jewish people to jealousy (see Rom. 11:11). Since *"the Jews require a sign,"* the way to provoke them to jealousy is through a demonstration of miracles.

Kathryn Kuhlman—a *normal* Christian who moved in miracles—foresaw a day when *normal* Christians would go into hospitals and empty them.

William Branham also saw this coming. He was the most accurate prophet of the 20th century. He had a vision of a giant tent. Lame, blind, and deaf people would walk into the tent with their infirmities and walk out the back of the tent instantly healed.

We are entering a time in history when the average Christian will move in supernatural power. This will bring about the fulfillment of Jesus' words: *"The works that I do he will do also; and greater works than these he will do"* (John 14:12 NKJV). Get ready for the greater works.

As you read about this amazing verified healing of Delores Winder, I believe the Holy Spirit will bubble up inside of you to become a *normal* Christian. I also expect many of you to receive healing in your own bodies because of the power of the testimony. The miracle healing anointing will literally splash off the pages.

Get ready to be part of the Elijah generation—the One New Man—and to move in the miraculous. As Mordecai said to Esther (a type of the end-time Church):

Yet who knows whether you have come to the kingdom for such a time as this? (Esther 4:14 NKJV).

Sid Roth, Host
It's Supernatural! Television Program

INTRODUCTION
BY BILL KEITH

The Lord your God is with you, He is mighty to save.
He will take great delight in you,
He will quiet you with His love,
He will rejoice over you with singing
(Zephaniah 3:17).

Delores Winder suffered as the victim of an incurable illness for 19½ years. She endured a disease known as pseudo-arthrosis, for which there is no known medical cure. This disease prevented her bones from absorbing those elements from the bloodstream essential for good health, and caused her bones to become dry and brittle. The end result of the disease is the development of acute osteoporosis, a condition which normally occurs in old age. For 15 years, Delores's activity was severely restricted by her body cast, which was used to support her deteriorating spine.

A battery of physicians and surgeons valiantly struggled to help Delores during the 19½ years of her illness. In attempts to mend her vertebrae so that she could sit up, walk, and carry on a normal life, the doctors performed four spinal fusions. Each fusion held for a time but ultimately failed as her physical condition continued to deteriorate.

Because of this deterioration, Delores was in constant pain and required increasing doses of pain medication in order to perform even the simplest tasks. For years she lived on tranquilizers and pain medication, but as she approached death, even the painkillers brought no relief.

Ultimately, when no further physical interventions would help Delores, the surgeons performed two percutaneous cordotomies, surgical procedures that destroy spinal nerves. These are procedures reserved for terminal patients to relieve their pain.

The surgeons explained to Delores that once the cordotomies were performed, the procedures would be irreversible. They told her that she would permanently lose feeling in most of her body, resulting in her inability to sense a burn or a cut on her body. She would also lose control of her body functions. Obviously, this was not an operation that one would choose unless in severe pain and near death. The surgeons performed a first, and then a second cordotomy, burning the nerve centers and severing the spinal cord segments. Delores's pain was relieved because the feeling in most of her body was gone.

As her illness reached its final stages, one of Delores's kidneys failed and the other became badly infected. Her esophagus had ruptured and her bowels had not moved in weeks. Her cardiopulmonary system was near collapse.

As Delores and her husband, Bill, began making her funeral arrangements, God moved in her life. During a 15-minute period on August 30, 1975, while attending a Methodist conference on the Holy Spirit in Dallas, Texas, where Kathryn Kuhlman was ministering, God completely healed Delores Winder. After that miracle, God called Delores to minister spiritual, emotional, and physical healing to His people.

The Delores Winder story will make you laugh and it will make you cry. Following her ministry across America is like walking through a new chapter of the Book of Acts. Her healing from the terminal illness undoubtedly was one of the great miracles of the 20th century. *Surprised by Healing* is her story. May it be used to set thousands of others free from their bondage to sickness and sin.

Bill Keith

Chapter 1

THE SHADOW OF DEATH

Even though I walk
through the valley of the shadow of death,
I will fear no evil,
for You are with me…
(Psalm 23:4).

The doctors said I was going to die. I had been sick for 19½ years and every minute of it showed on my body. I had stalled the Judgment Day for nearly two decades, but my time was running out. After all those years of sickness and pain, I had begun to hope that all my illness would do was kill me. Dying would be easy; enduring more pain was unthinkable.

For months death had stalked me, casting its shadow over my emaciated body. A lot of people truly believe they will live forever, but I had to accept the fact that forever was something I no longer could offer anyone.

My life during those 19½ years had been a preview of hell. Thank God I was a Christian and knew I was going to Heaven where I would finally be free of the body cast and neck brace that had burdened me; free of hospitals, surgeries, pain, and medication; and free of all torment. Free to walk and run again.

"Maybe, God, I'll get the feeling back in my legs! And in my arms and body!" I often dreamed out loud. "Oh, it would be so nice to feel someone's arms around me again," I thought, "Perhaps the arms of Jesus." I wondered what it would be like to go somewhere alone again. You forget freedom after 19½ years of being an invalid.

My husband Bill and our teenage son Chris were kind to me and helpful. Our married son Doug, his wife Ann, and our three grandchildren lived nearby and helped me so much. They were the epitome of kindness and love, but how wonderful it would have been to do something by myself again. The confinement of my illness had been difficult for me because I had been so fiercely independent and active.

An Incurable Ailment

My doctors called my illness, which had begun in 1956, *pseudoarthrosis* and told me that there was no known cure or any way to stop its progression. The only option was to live and die with it. They explained that a healthy person's bloodstream contains everything necessary to keep the bones strong; but in my case, my bones did not absorb what they needed from my bloodstream. As a result, I developed advanced osteoporosis, causing my bones to become old and brittle long before their time.

I was hospitalized from January through April of 1957, when the doctors discovered that the osteoporosis was causing the bones in my back to deteriorate. During my hospital stay, surgeons performed the first of my spinal fusions, an operation that was intended to hold my crumbling vertebrae in place. The doctors used bone for the fusion taken from the larger of the two bones in my leg. I was put in a back brace to support my spine and told that I would never be without it again.

Yet, even the brace didn't provide enough support, and I had to walk bent over to keep my spine from getting caught on some bone spurs that had developed at the spinal fusion sites. If I were not careful, these spurs would pull down more of the vertebrae in my already weakened back.

Bill built me a special steel brace for support. It worked for a while, but had to be worn outside my clothing. The steel supports stuck out at the sides, and as I walked around the house, Bill, Chris, and our friend John Andrews would hang dishtowels on the end of my brace, to ease the tension. We would all laugh about it.

Someone once asked one of my friends, "How could you be so cruel as to joke about Delores's illness?"

"That's the only way we could live with it," the friend replied. Bill often joked about feeding me Elmer's Glue in order to hold me together. Bill and Chris would ask, "How much Elmer's Glue do you think it would take to hold Mama together?" My dear, wonderful Bill, who stood faithfully with me during all those painful years, once said, "We have to joke about it to keep from crying."

Surgery and More Surgery

After the spinal fusion, our family had to make quite a lot of adjustments. I couldn't drive our car because the doctor told me that even pushing down on the brake pedal could send my back into shock and break more vertebrae. But at this early point in my illness, I could still take part in the care of my family.

I managed fairly well for two-and-a-half years, until the first fusion broke. The doctors then repeated the fusion using a graft from the other leg and put me in a body cast from under my arms down to my legs. During the next 15 years, the doctors would perform two additional spinal fusions.

Because none of the three previous fusions lasted, the doctors decided to perform the fourth one through the front. This frontal fusion was an attempt to bond my crumbling bone to the front of the vertebrae. The surgery was just unbelievable. Once the incision was made, the surgeons had to remove all the vital organs in the area in order to insert the bone. After fusing the bone, they put all my organs back in and closed the incision. A nurse at the hospital later told me that the doctor ordered her to check me every hour after the surgery stating that, "He didn't want me lying there dead in a hospital bed."

The frontal fusion held for only a short time and then my condition grew rapidly worse. The pain became unbearable. The doctors' next step was to perform a percutaneous cordotomy, a procedure that would control the pain, but was usually reserved for terminal patients.

Prior to the cordotomy, the doctors offered me a clear explanation of what the operation meant. They told me that *percutaneous cordotomy* literally means burning out the nerve centers in the spinal column and that, once destroyed, the nerve centers could not be restored again. This procedure would have permanent consequences.

Although the doctors tried not to be blunt about it, the unmistakable implication was that the cordotomy was being performed only because there was no hope of curing my disease; I was dying. The cordotomy would give me some relief during the final stages of my illness.

The surgeons also carefully explained that the procedure would involve burning at least six spinal cord segments above the origin of the pain. In order to achieve complete pain relief, the entire lateral spinothalamic tract would have to be burned through. If it were not, the pain would remain.

They did not open me up surgically, but simply inserted a needle through my skin, and then into the spinal cord using x-ray to guide them. The doctors then literally burned the nerve centers, destroying them completely. The procedure was a great success because the pain was gone, but afterwards I had no feeling from the neck level down on my right side. As a result, I couldn't lift my feet off the floor. However, I was able to walk a little by shuffling my legs.

Over the next year and a half, the pain increased so much on the left side of my body that the doctors decided to perform another cordotomy. Once again, they explained to me that once the nerve centers from the left side of my body were destroyed the procedure would be irreversible and nerve function could never be restored.

They again went back into the spinal column, burning out all the nerve centers on my left side, as far up the spine as they could—about three inches above my waist. They couldn't go higher because my heart and lungs were in such bad condition from wearing the body cast all those years and also because my body was weak from inactivity. The second cordotomy was also a great success; I felt no pain on the left side in the areas that were deadened. However, I still had pain in other parts of my body.

When you try to walk with bilateral cordotomies affecting both legs, you have to watch your feet very carefully. Your brain has to tell your legs to move since you have no feeling in your feet. You can't lift your feet, but you can shuffle them along. The doctors didn't even know that a person with two cordotomies could shuffle until they saw me do it.

The surgeon told me, "Delores, you will probably be in a wheelchair from now on, because we've never known a person with two cordotomies who ever walked again." The day after the second cordotomy, I told my doctors, "I want up; I'm going to walk." And I "walked" in my shuffling fashion.

Talk about the chains that satan puts around you—my whole body had the signature of satan written all over it. And when he catches you in a trap, he isn't about to let you go.

An Ailing Spirit

Along with all my physical problems, I also had a spiritual problem of which I was aware. Oh, I knew Jesus, but He was in Heaven. And I knew about satan, but I thought he was in hell. I read my Bible and would say that I believed it to be the infallible Word of God. I knew it was the truth. Yet because of my church upbringing, I put healing and deliverance back in the apostolic age. I believed these things were "not for today." The only time I ever heard the term *Holy Spirit* was when we recited the Apostles' Creed at church—and it had been a long time since I had been able to go to church.

Although I knew that I was a Christian and was going to Heaven, I always seemed to be looking for something more. Before my illness began, my husband Bill and I worked with the young people in our Methodist church. It was so frustrating when those kids would come to me with problems for which there seemed to be no answers. We just encouraged them to try to be good, to attend church and do their best. We would tell them, "We'll pray for you," but never said, "We'll pray with you." One day I cried out, "Dear God, there must be more to give young people than this!"

Our minister didn't have any answers either. While he was visiting me one day, I asked, "What else is there?"

"What do you mean, 'What else is there?'" he asked.

"Where did the excitement of being a Christian go?" I asked.

"Delores, you're always hunting for something you don't have," he replied.

It troubled me when I read the Bible and saw that the New Testament Christians were excited, but here we were doing our Christian "chores" and nothing ever happened. Day after day I read the Bible and would think, "Wouldn't it have been nice to have lived when Jesus walked here on the earth? So many things happened. Was it only for those three short years of His ministry and for the disciples and apostles who had walked with Him? When He was here there were miracles. Why?"

I felt as though I had a giant jigsaw puzzle of Christianity with a great big piece missing and no one—not even my minister—could tell me what the missing piece was.

A Welcomed Death Sentence

In the spring of 1975, I went back into the hospital. It had become a constant battle just to keep my body functioning. One of my kidneys had closed and the other carried a constant infection. My bowels had not moved in several weeks and my stomach had troubled me from the time I first entered the body cast 15 years earlier. Also, my esophagus had ruptured.

My doctors kept me doped up all the time in an attempt to kill the increasing pain, but it wasn't working very well. When the pain became unbearable, they gave me stronger painkillers. I was living on pills to tranquilize me, pills for my ruptured esophagus, pills for my stomach, pills for my kidneys, pills for my heart, pills for low blood pressure, and pills to sleep. My whole world seemed to revolve around those little bottles of pills.

All I could eat was dry toast, a cup of tea, a small piece of broiled chicken, and instant chicken noodle soup from a package. No wonder my invalid body weight dropped to 73 pounds. The doctors asked me to go into the hospital for some additional tests to determine if there was anything further that could be done for me medically.

Dr. I.L. Van Zandt, who had treated me for nine years, was a very compassionate man. We became close friends. He had gone through a lot of trauma in his own life and often shared his feelings with me. He found me to be a good listener. Why not? There wasn't much else for me to do. But Van and the other doctors had lost hope; they knew I was dying and that it was just a matter of time.

My doctors had kind hearts. Before they finally gave up hope, they decided to call in another neurosurgeon to see if there was anything further that could be done for me. The neurosurgeon examined me thoroughly and told Van it was time for my body to die.

It was Van's unhappy duty to tell me the results of the final tests the neurosurgeon had conducted. He had told Van that a person's body can only tolerate so much disease, illness, and pain. Van really didn't have to tell me the results of the tests. A person knows when her body is dying. I actually looked forward to it.

Van came into my room, walked over to the bed, and said, "Delores, I'm sorry. There's nothing else that can be done." I looked up at that kind doctor and tried to smile. "Your body has just taken all it can endure—it's time to die," he said, with a distraught, sad expression on his face.

"Don't, Van. Don't be sorry," I told him. "I'm going to be out of this hell soon and I'll be free. It's official and I'm glad."

"Delores, I would do anything in the world to make you well and I can't do a thing," he said. Then, after a long pause, he added, "Even the tissues in your back are shredding."

He explained that some of the muscles in my back had dropped and caused my bowels to cease functioning. My body was preparing for death. Then he left. During the next few days I tried to adjust to the idea of dying soon.

The second week in July, after Chris's 14th birthday, we carefully planned my funeral. I tagged my jewelry and the little things I wanted to leave for my loved ones. About all that was left for me to do was wait.

Except for one little hitch.

Chapter 2

DAYS OF ANGUISH

The Sovereign Lord is my strength;
He makes my feet like the feet of a deer,
He enables me to go on the heights
(Habakkuk 3:19).

Before Bill moved us to Texas in 1958, God had given us a baby. We already had our teenage sons, Doug and Mike, and had not expected our family to increase.

While we were living in Oregon, God worked out circumstances that allowed me to become acquainted with a certain woman. One morning at about 2 A.M., she called on the phone and was crying.

"Delores, I'm going to have a baby," she said, sobbing.

"Well, that's not so bad," I replied. "It happens all the time."

"But I can't keep it; I can't raise the child," she said. "I want that child in the best Christian home I know—and that's yours and Bill's. Will you take the baby?"

"Why, of course," I answered.

We talked for another hour, then I hung up the phone and prepared to go back to sleep.

"Who was that?" Bill asked, and I told him.

"What did she want?" he asked.

"To give us a baby," I replied.

"Oh," he said, turning over in bed to go back to sleep.

A few minutes later, he jumped up in bed and yelled, "What did you say?"

"Forget it, Bill," I replied. "She just found out she's pregnant and wants us to take the baby, but she'll decide to keep it."

But from that time on it was our baby. When my friend would discuss the child she was carrying, she would refer to it as "your baby." She completely disassociated herself from the child because she knew she couldn't keep it.

Before the baby was born, it was settled that the judge would grant the adoption because a foster child had done so well in our home.

The baby was such a precious little fella. Immediately we loved him as our own. We named him *Christopher*, meaning "Christ bearer." How appropriate that name was, because he was the instrument of God's light in my life. Shortly after the adoption, Bill decided we would move to Arlington, Texas.

The Toll on Our Son

The day after we left for Texas, I knew my fusion had broken. The doctors had told me that if the fusion broke, I could not walk. If I couldn't walk, how could I take care of my family, particularly little Chris? There was only a slight nagging pain in my back, but I knew the fusion was broken. Yet I was still walking.

The first thing we did when we arrived in Texas was to find a doctor. He confirmed that the fusion was shattered. Although little Chris was less than three months old, the doctor placed me on experimental medication for seven months, hoping the fusion would mend. Throughout the seven months, it was necessary for others to take care of our new baby. Thank God for good neighbors and for family.

Before entering the hospital for the second fusion, I prayed, "God, help me to bear this." He did. God, who hears our prayers and answers us, gave me exactly what I asked of Him. It wasn't God's fault that I didn't know what the Word said about His promises to heal my body. After all, I had read the Bible, I had taught Sunday school for many years, and I had grown up in church. I wasn't dumb—just blind to the truth of the Word.

The second fusion proved not to be the answer, for they had to place me in a body cast with more restrictions, and more pain.

Now there was the added grief of having a child barely a year old and not being able to care for him. It was at this point that I began to question God.

I would ask, "God, why? Why did You give this child to us? He has spent three months with grandparents he didn't even know, all the while crying for me and not understanding why I deserted him."

Yet that was only the beginning for Chris. He would have to endure years and years of that kind of life. There were so many people helping him and telling him what to do; but all of them had different ideas about what was correct. He didn't understand what was happening and became nervous, anxious, and uncertain of both himself and us. I too became uncertain and would repeatedly ask, "God, where are You?"

Misery was all that little Chris knew during the first five years of his life. He saw his mother in bed, always suffering, with bottles of pills everywhere. Chris never knew me without a body cast.

Reasons to Live

As the years passed, we worked out some semblance of a normal family life. I could get out of bed a bit and Bill was able to go to work. Our good friend and neighbor, Betty, would spend time with Chris and me. She taught Chris to draw pictures. Betty was Japanese. She was such a blessing to us with her quiet, loving nature.

As the pain grew worse, Dr. Mycoskie, my first doctor in Arlington, started injections into my spine. Sometimes his nurse would come to the parking lot and give me a shot of Demerol so that they could settle me down enough to get me out of the car and into his office. If I tried to hold out a day too long to receive the shots of Demerol, I paid dearly through the increased pain.

One day I realized my legs were getting numb. I kept quiet about it, but I knew that our time of family stability was just about over. The pain was so bad that Bill had to improvise a bed for me.

He took an old army cot, stripped it, and then used webbing placed so that my spine was as free as possible, not touching anything.

The new bed, along with the increase in shots up and down the spinal area, provided some comfort, but even that didn't last.

It was a vicious cycle of pain, hospitals, bills, concern for Chris, wondering how long it could go on, and then finally learning that the end was near. One day, after my last hospital visit in 1975, I was talking to my neighbor Betty about dying. She said to me, "No, you have big power in you. I don't understand it, but you'll not die." I was too exhausted to tell her that all I wanted was to go on to Heaven and be free of the suffering of this life.

Our Methodist minister was no longer coming to see me, but in all fairness, who wouldn't have tired of the hopeless situation that was mine? A Presbyterian minister continued to come regularly and tried to bring as much comfort as possible to us. He became my new pastor and I wanted him to preach my funeral.

But thoughts of Chris kept flashing through my mind and I found myself thinking, "God, just one more year and perhaps he will be old enough to survive." I kept getting what I asked for—one more year at a time. As a matter of fact, I always got what I asked for from God—but that was all I asked, all that I knew to ask.

Caught in a Trap

Sometimes fighting for life was so painful and seemed so futile; but then the thought of our young Chris getting ready to lose his mother would put some fight back in me. Eventually, the fight was just about gone. When the doctors told me my heart had stopped beating during the frontal surgery, I thought, "Why didn't I die?" At other times I would think, "God, I'm caught in a trap. What is the answer? I cannot live in this pain, and I can't die."

Of course the answer was simple—Jesus heals. But no one had told me about that. I believed the Lord for my salvation and knew He would help me over the rough places, but the churches we attended had taught that healing had been for the apostolic age. We were taught that today healing comes through medicine, surgery, and doctors. "Only fanatics," I was told, "still believe in healing other than through surgery, medicine, and doctors." As a result, I wasn't healed.

As the deterioration became worse, the disease spread completely up my spine, skipped three vertebrae at the top, and then went into my neck. The pain was severe. Then one day I fell, which caused further pain and deterioration. At that point, I could no longer hold up my head, so the doctors provided me with a big Queen Anne (medical) collar.

The osteoporosis spread across my shoulders and into my wrists, even down to my fingers. I could no longer pick up anything with my fingers without feeling pain. At times, my wrists would come out of their joints. The doctors taught Bill how to put my wrists back into place when they popped out. Even after Bill snapped my wrists back, I had to wear an elastic bandage around them for days until the joints would hold.

A Family's Cries

We tried as a family to spend one hour a day together in the den in our home talking, laughing, even playing games, or at least trying to. Some days I couldn't stand the pain, and Bill would carry me back to bed.

Chris was unstable and uptight, having gone through all his life watching his mother slowly dying. Each afternoon when he returned home from school, he would shout, "Mother!" wondering if I had made it through the day. If I was asleep and didn't answer him immediately, he panicked and screamed, running through the house and into my bedroom.

Once when he was five, I remained in the hospital for so long that he thought I had died and that Bill and Doug were keeping the news from him. When they brought me home, Chris almost collapsed. He had made up his mind that he would never see me again.

His mother was a person he had never seen out of a body cast…a mother who hardly ever visited his school…a mother he couldn't hug because he might hurt her or cause her more pain—and now a mother who soon would be leaving him forever.

One day I told a minister who came for a visit, "I don't understand this thing with Chris at all. This is not my kind of God who would let a child suffer like this."

The minister reflected on the statement for a while, then replied, "Delores, look at the strength He's putting into that boy."

"Dear Lord," I thought. "How much strength does a little boy need? How much does he have to see and how much does he have to suffer to be strong?"

There were times when my heart became so weak that it would almost stop beating. Immediately, I would think, "This is it." Then I would take a couple of deep breaths and it would start beating regularly again. I almost dreaded the return of the pounding in my chest because I so wanted to die.

At times I would hold my breath for long periods of time. I thought that if I held my breath long enough, my weakened heart would stop. But always, just before it stopped, the thought of a motherless Chris flashed through my mind, and I would start breathing again.

One evening I heard Chris crying. I shuffled into his room to find out what was wrong. He looked up at me with huge tears in his eyes and said, "You're dying, aren't you, Mother?"

"Yes, Chris, but everyone is," I replied.

"No, I mean now," he said.

"Yes, I am," I answered, almost hesitantly. "Chris, if you cry that is all we'll remember. But if we try to enjoy each day, you'll have some pleasant memories." He didn't seem to understand.

"Chris, can't you be happy for me?" I asked him. "You've never seen me any other way and now it's time for me to go home to Heaven where I won't be like this anymore. Can't you be happy for that?"

Answering as a 14-year-old would, he said, "But what about me? I can be happy for you; but what is going to happen to me? How will I feel coming home from school with you not here?"

His question stunned me. It bothered me that I had nothing to give to Chris for strength and courage. The thought occurred to me that I could say, "Chris, you can pray." To a 14-year-old about to lose his mother, however, that wouldn't mean very much. He had prayed for me from the time Bill and I first taught him to pray and hadn't seen any answers.

Chris was like a wound-up spring. He was so nervous that he bit his fingernails down to the quick. I was afraid that when I died he would snap emotionally and no one would ever be able to put him back together again. That day I prayed, "God, You are going to have to show me something that will save Chris. Show me that when I'm gone he will be alright." On another occasion I broke down and wept, crying out to God, "You've got to give me some assurance that Chris is not going to fall apart."

God Was There

There had been times through the years when I thought the pain could be endured no longer. Often I would dump a bunch of pills into my hand, thinking I would take them all at once and just go ahead and end my useless, helpless life, but the thought of Chris always stopped me. How could he accept a suicide in addition to all the other heartaches he had to endure? I would put the pills back into the bottles.

Even in the midst of all the physical suffering and anguish over Chris, God was good to me. There were times when I lay in bed in wracking pain so intense that even the painkillers would bring no relief.

During some of the worst times, I would rise above the pain by imagining myself in the mountains or by the sea watching the tide roll in and out. I would picture myself sitting on top of the mountain looking across a valley to another mountain high above a little ribbon of a river flowing down through the valley. I could even see wildflowers growing in clumps near where I was sitting. The mountains were so beautiful. As my mind wandered far away to the mountains, the little river, and the wildflowers, the pain would go away for a while.

Or I could imagine sitting on a piece of driftwood by the seaside, watching the waves come in and listening to the sound of the water.

When you are bedfast, you learn to appreciate those little things that seem relatively unimportant in a busy world: a child laughing, a baby crying, a teenager walking carefree down the street, a child wanting to love you even though you're wearing a cast.

Children are often afraid of the grotesque, including strange-looking people in large body casts who can't run and play with them. Yet we rarely found a child who was afraid to come near me. Instead, children would come up and want to feel the cast. One child rapped on my cast and said, "Are you in there?" making a joyful game out of it. It made me laugh, too.

We had friends who came to see me nearly every day. Some would come for a while then never return, unable to cope with seeing me in such pain. Some people can't handle another person's lengthy illness. They go through so much with you that it drains their emotions.

During those final days I just settled back and waited, hoping the end would come soon. When all hope was finally gone, God decided to step in and take over.

Chapter 3

STRANGE AND WONDERFUL WAYS

"For My thoughts are not your thoughts,
neither are your ways My ways,"
declares the Lord
(Isaiah 55:8).

One Sunday morning God sent a woman named Velma Despain to see me. She lived in our neighborhood, but had never visited in our home. Her daughter, Gail Bond, lived close by and helped take care of me. Gail had told her mother to stay away from me because her mother belonged to the Assemblies of God church and people thought she was a little weird.

Gail had told her mother, "I don't want you bothering Delores; she is too sick." So her mother never came to see me, although we lived in the same neighborhood. But on that particular Sunday, Velma came into my home and went back to the bedroom without Bill knowing.

I was having church in bed that morning, watching a worship service on television. Before we had time to exchange pleasantries, Velma walked over and switched the channel on my television set. The next thing I saw was a woman seemingly floating out onto the stage in a flowing gown, saying very dramatically, *"I believe in miracles!"*

I took one look at the rather strange-looking woman who invaded the relative quiet of my inner sanctum via the television screen, and somewhat caustically asked, "Who's that?"

Velma smiled and replied, "That's Kathryn Kuhlman."

"Turn her off!" I ordered.

"Don't you ever watch her program?" Velma asked.

"No! Turn her off!" I exclaimed.

A Troubling Question Answered

I had grown up in Johnstown, Pennsylvania, and knew all about Kathryn Kuhlman, the so-called "faith healer." In Johnstown we referred to her as, "That kook who says she heals people." The newspapers had exposed her, doctors had exposed her, and everyone knew she was a fake, didn't they? I even remembered our Methodist preacher telling us to stay away from her when she came to our area for one of her healing meetings. Being a good Methodist woman, I stayed away.

Although I personally had never heard Kathryn Kuhlman, when I saw her on television that morning it was even worse than I had thought. Velma reached over and flipped the television channel away from the Kathryn Kuhlman program and I felt an immediate sense of relief.

"Why don't you watch Miss Kuhlman?" Velma asked.

"Because I don't like her," I shot back.

Although I was being rude to Velma, she kept smiling. She didn't say another word until it was time for her to return home. Suddenly she said, "Good-bye," and started toward the door. Then she turned, looked me straight in the eye, and asked, "What if you are closing a door to God?"

"By not watching Kathryn Kuhlman? That's ridiculous!" I laughed. Velma left the room, but her question remained with me. At first the question only troubled me a little; but later, it disturbed me a lot. It kept nagging at me. After all, I was begging God to give me an answer about Chris. Sometime later, Velma told me that she was not even aware that she had asked me the question and didn't know why she had come to visit me that day.

That very day, bewildered by the troublesome question Velma had posed, I prayed and said, "God, if I can open a door by watching Kathryn Kuhlman, I'll do it. But You must tell me; otherwise I don't want to watch her." It was sometime later that I realized *that* prayer marked the first time I had ever told God I needed to hear from Him.

My prayers had always been like most other people's, something like, "God, if it's Your will," or "God, I'm having another surgery and would like to be well."

How many ministers had prayed simple prayers for me through the years? Prayers like, "Lord, give Delores the strength to endure." And I endured.

For two more days, I prayed about watching the Kathryn Kuhlman program, yet nothing happened. I thought the windows of Heaven were closed to me. Since I heard nothing from God on the matter, I decided it wasn't necessary for me to watch her program. But God sneaked up on me.

Having undergone two percutaneous cordotomies, I had no control over my body functions, and therefore I never knew when I needed to use the bathroom. I set up a schedule to remind me to go at certain intervals, but often I would have an "accident" during the night and would wake up in a wet bed. One morning I woke up and the bed was completely dry. I couldn't understand why, but since Gail hadn't arrived yet, I decided to get up and go to the bathroom by myself.

Bill had erected a monkey bar over my bed, and I used it to move around a little from time to time. That morning, I grabbed the monkey bar and tried to pull myself up into a sitting position in order to move toward the bathroom. As I did, a sudden pain hit my shoulder, shot through my neck, and into my head. I thought my brain had exploded.

I fell back down in the bed in great agony; but as I fell back, I distinctly heard a clear voice say the words *Kathryn Kuhlman*. I heard only her name, nothing else.

That really threw me for a loop, and I yelled, "Gail!" But Gail didn't answer.

A few minutes later, Gail came in, looked at me, and said, "You're awfully quiet."

"Gail, were you here a little while ago?" I asked.

"No," she answered.

"Gail, I heard someone say Kathryn Kuhlman's name," I told her.

She laughed and said, "You told God He would have to answer your prayer. Maybe you should watch her program."

"Well, maybe I will," I agreed.

God's Opportunity Knocks

The next day, Gail's mother, Velma, came back to see me. She was on her way to California for a visit and just dropped by to see how I was doing.

"Delores, Kathryn Kuhlman is going to be in Dallas at the end of the month," she said. "If you are interested in going to hear her, here are the phone numbers to call for reservations."

I took the piece of paper with the phone numbers written on it, all the time thinking, "Why am I taking this? I won't even be alive at the end of this month. This Velma is really flaky."

After Velma left, I picked up the phone, called the number she had given me, and ordered two tickets for the meeting. The tickets never came. The doctors had me so doped up that I never knew why the tickets weren't mailed to us. Perhaps the people on the phone told me to send a check and I just didn't remember.

It was August 1975. Knowing I was dying, several friends and family members from up north came for a last visit. Because I was so weak, it took all the energy I had just to visit with them.

Because we had so much company in the house and because I never knew one day from another, I didn't get a chance to watch Kathryn Kuhlman's television program that Sunday or the next.

In my weakened and confused state, I began to think again that it would be easy to die if I helped a little, but somehow I managed to hang on to life. Then God started moving again.

The end of the month came and I was still barely alive. It finally dawned on me that I had never received the Kathryn Kuhlman tickets. "Oh, well," I thought, "God didn't want me to go, anyway." At that time I didn't realize that we have an enemy who tries to stop us from doing those things God wants us to do.

A few days later, for some unknown reason, Velma's husband called her in California and told her to come home. When Velma asked why, he said, "I just want you home."

"I had planned to return next week," she argued.

"No, I want you home tomorrow," he said emphatically.

Velma was strong-willed. Although she was fuming, she boarded a jet and immediately returned to Dallas. She arrived home on Friday. Her daughter Gail went to the airport to meet her. Before Gail left for the airport, she told me, "I hate having to go pick up Mother right now; she's going to be mad about having to come home." She was.

The next morning Velma happened to call her 83-year-old Aunt Ruth in Dallas. The first question her aunt asked her was, "Did Delores get to go hear Kathryn Kuhlman?"

Velma, who had told her aunt about my illness said, "No."

Aunt Ruth then said, "I have one ticket for tonight and I know it's hers."

The elderly woman had wanted to call to offer me the ticket. However, she didn't know my last name and Gail didn't have a telephone. Although it didn't dawn on me at the time, one thing was very clear: Velma had to come home from California in order for me to get that ticket. God worked His will through many in order to get one person where He wanted her to be.

God's Outstretched Hand

Another amazing detail was that the meeting for which Aunt Ruth gave me a ticket was a Methodist conference on the Holy Spirit being held in the Dallas Convention Center. The Kathryn Kuhlman meeting for which I never received my ticket was a Full Gospel Businessmen's meeting.

Had I attended the Full Gospel Businessmen's meeting and seen someone with hands lifted in praise or who had shouted "Hallelujah," I would have split the door wide open getting out of there. To me, fanaticism just had no place in the church or among Christian people. The Methodist meeting, however, would be nice, quiet and orderly. No one would get excited or carried away.

Once I knew that I had a ticket, I had to tell Bill I wanted to go to the meeting. I asked him to come into the bedroom and said, "Bill, I've got to go to Dallas to hear Kathryn Kuhlman."

He looked at me rather strangely and asked, "Why?"

"Because I'm going to learn something that I need to know for Chris," I replied.

Bill, always a thinker, always full of logic, said, "How are you going to get there?"

"I don't know, but I have to go," I answered. He reluctantly agreed to let Gail take me.

On Saturday night, Gail helped him get me ready for the ride from Arlington to Dallas. Before we left, Bill told Gail, "Now when you get over there, she won't be able to go in, so just turn around and bring her home." He knew that it would be too painful for me to have to get out of the car, go into the convention hall, find a seat, and sit through the meeting.

Just as we were leaving, Chris came into the bedroom and said, "Mother, where are you going?"

"Chris, I have to go to Dallas," I replied.

"What for?" he asked.

"I have to go hear a woman speak," I answered.

"You must really like her," he said.

"No, I don't like her at all," I said.

"Then why are you going?" he asked.

"Because God is going to teach me something I need to know for you," I said.

"Mother, why don't you like her?" he asked.

"She's a woman I know about from Pennsylvania, and she's a woman who says she heals people," I told him.

"Mother! You're going to be healed," he said quietly.

Chris was all excited and his face just glowed. However, I felt that his words went too far; the child made what I thought was a foolish statement. I wanted to correct him so he wouldn't build up his hopes and then be disappointed when I returned home sick. Deciding to give him a good lecture, I said, "Chris, sit down." Obediently he sat on the side of the bed.

"That does not happen anymore," I told him. "There were healings when Jesus was here, and later with the disciples and apostles, but that was the end of healing. I don't want you thinking that I'm going to come home any different than I am now."

Then I added, "Except I'm going to learn something we need to know to help you. Do you understand?"

"Yes, ma'am," he said. Then it was time to go.

Bill carried me to the car and laid me down in the back seat where he earlier had made a bed out of blankets and pillows. The trip to Dallas took 25 minutes. Although the pain was severe, the hope of finding something from God that I could leave with Chris when I died helped me bear the pain.

When we arrived at the convention center, Gail pulled up in front of the entrance and parked. She turned around to me in the back seat and said, "Can you get out?"

"No," I replied. I was so weak that I could hardly keep my senses, let alone try to get into an auditorium.

"Well, we'll just go back home," Gail said, with a sound of relief in her voice.

Then the back door of the car opened and a man was standing there looking at me. He said, "Let me help you." Then he reached inside the back seat and lifted me out of the car. He told Gail to go park the car and said he would take care of me. "I'll keep her in the lobby until you get back," he said.

When Gail returned to the lobby, the kind man helped me shuffle into the auditorium where he located our seats and helped me sit down. He tried to make me comfortable, but of course that wasn't possible. I asked the man if he would bring me a cup of water so I could take my pain pills.

Chapter 4

RISE AND BE HEALED

When Jesus saw her,
He called her forward and said to her,
"Woman, you are set free from your infirmity."
Then He put His hands on her,
and immediately she straightened up and praised God
(Luke 13:12-13).

The big event of the Methodist conference on the Holy Spirit that Saturday night of August 30, 1975, was the appearance of Kathryn Kuhlman. She floated out on stage, her long gown flowing with her, a big smile on her face. And just as I had seen her on television, she said quite dramatically, *"I believe in miracles!"*

I took one look at the show and said, "Dear Lord, what am I doing here?" All of my negative feelings about Kathryn Kuhlman rose up within me again. I couldn't even stand to be in the same auditorium with her. Then an inner voice spoke to me, "Now you came here to learn something. You don't have to look at her to learn it."

"Sure," I thought, "I won't learn anything by watching her." Besides, I had on a neck brace and a cast and couldn't hold up my head.

I looked up at her only twice during the entire evening. But oh, did I learn something!

As she spoke, she introduced me to a God I didn't know. She talked about the Holy Spirit and even called it *He.* She said, "He is the third person of the Trinity."

"Why does she keep calling the Holy Spirit *He?*" I asked myself. Then she told the audience that if we were still referring to the Holy Spirit as *it,* we didn't really know Him.

While she talked about the Holy Spirit coming to be with us and explained that He was the very presence of God with us doing the work Jesus did, I knew His presence for the first time in my life. I felt it behind me and around the sides of me. If I had reached out my hand, I could have touched Him.

Although I don't remember exactly what Kathryn Kuhlman said, it was something like, "Do you know Him? If you don't know Him, why don't you know Him? Jesus was so certain of the Holy Spirit and the work He would do that He was able and ready to die for us. Jesus knew the Holy Spirit would come to continue His work; He knew the Holy Spirit would never leave you or forsake you."

I was afraid, but I knew I was feeling the presence of God. As I became aware that I was meeting God in the service that night, I found myself open to Him. He was not sitting way up on His throne some-where. He was right there with me. Sitting there listening to Kathryn Kuhlman speak, the Lord opened up my mind and told me what I needed to do for Chris.

As I felt the presence of the Lord around me I closed my eyes, hop-ing to shut out everything but the awareness of Him. Behind my closed eyes, I saw Chris standing on our front porch; he was not alone. There was a man standing beside him. Then I heard the man speak, saying, "Tell Chris he need never walk into the house alone. Tell him to close his eyes and picture Jesus, then reach out and take My hand. I'll walk with him. My name is *Holy Spirit.*"

I knew with certainty that I had heard the Lord speak to me. He gave me the answer to what would become of Bill and Chris and the rest of my family after I was gone. "Lord, it is so simple," I said. "Please don't let me forget this before I get home." I feared forgetting it all because of the heavy doses of medication I was taking.

"That's what I came to learn. Now I'm ready to go home," I said to myself as joy flooded through my heart. "Oh, thank You, Lord. Chris will never be alone. He will never have to walk into the house alone without You there." That was the answer. God had given me the answer. In my mind I could picture Chris coming home alone. Now I could tell him, "Just stand quietly for a minute and reach out and take His hand and walk into that house with Him."

I had received an intimate revelation. By this time in the service, my head was aching so badly that it actually felt like it would blow up. "I wish she would stop talking now so we can go home," I thought.

A Miracle in the Balance

In what seemed like an answer to my prayer, Kathryn Kuhlman stopped talking and started praying. As she began to pray, I thought, "Lord, You are so good. It's just about over." Every part of me that could hurt was hurting. My body was pounding and throbbing with pain so intense I wanted to scream.

Then she stopped praying and said, "Someone out there just had an ear opened. If you'll come up here, you'll receive your healing."

A man stood up and walked toward the platform and up the stairs to Kathryn Kuhlman. Several other people followed him. She walked around behind the man. In her stage whisper (which was almost as loud as my voice), she said, "Can you hear me?"

I thought, "Sure he can hear her. I can hear her clear back here."

Then the man replied, "Yes, I can hear you! I can hear you!"

"Well that's just great; everybody in here can hear you," I thought, never believing that man had been deaf. "Why shouldn't he hear you?"

Then several of the other people who had followed the man up to the platform started jumping up and down, each one of them saying, "I can hear! I can hear!"

"What is going on in here?" I wondered.

Then Kathryn Kuhlman walked up in front of that man. When she touched him, he fell on the floor. I couldn't believe my eyes. "Why did she knock him down?" I asked. Then she went to all the other people and started knocking them down.

When she approached a really big man, I said, "She won't be able to knock him down." But when she touched the big man, he hit the floor. "She couldn't have knocked him down," I reasoned. "Oh, I know. Pressure points. She's hitting pressure points."

Then a voice said to me, "Get out of here. She's making a mockery of God. Why does God allow her to do that?"

"Boy, that's right," I said. "Here she introduced me to the living God, and now she has a sideshow going on up there." I was mad.

Again the voice said, "Get out of here." I really wanted to get out.

I turned to Gail and said, "Let's go." Her face was as white as a sheet. Her eyes were as big as silver dollars as she nodded, unable to speak. Gail bent over to pick up some things off the floor and handed me my cane.

Using the cane, I started moving myself to the front of the seat so she could get hold of me and get me out of there quickly. "God, let me get out of here and don't let any of them nab me," I prayed.

I was scared and making every effort to move as fast as I could. Then I realized that the tops of my legs were on fire. It was so painful I had to bite my lips in order to inch my way to the front of the seat. I looked down at my legs and thought, "I'm glad I only have to wear my cast one hour a day now. It's making my legs burn." I had to clasp my legs together to keep myself from screaming.

Finally I reached the edge of the seat and waited for Gail to get hold of me and get me out of that crazy place.

Then someone said to me, "Why do you have on that neck brace?" I looked around and there was a man crouched down by my chair.

"I have a bad neck," I answered, and turned away from him.

After a brief pause, he said, "But something is happening to you."

"Yes. My legs are burning like crazy," I replied.

Then he said, "Would you like to walk with me?"

"Yes. Get me out of here," I replied. He nodded and helped me up. In my heart, I knew the Lord had sent the man to get me out of that place.

Realizing I couldn't walk he said, "How can I help you?"

"If you put one arm around me and then hold my arm, I can shuffle," I said.

I was just about in glory knowing he was getting me out of there and no one was going to stop us. As we started out, he began asking me questions. Questions annoyed me and I always had a smart answer. When you're an invalid, you become very clever at shutting people up.

He asked, "Have you had surgery?"

"I've had four fusions and two percutaneous cordotomies," I replied. When I used the words *percutaneous cordotomies*, it usually shut people up for good.

He stopped, turned me around to face him, and said, "You've had two percutaneous cordotomies and your legs are burning? Isn't that rather strange?"

"He knows what I'm talking about," I thought. "Yes," I answered, but I decided not to say anything more to him. We started toward the door again, and after a struggle, he led me to the door that opened into the lobby. He still had his arm around me as I used the cane to steady myself as I shuffled along.

When we got to the door, he said, "I know you don't know what is happening to you, but you can take off your cast if you want to."

"My God! These people are dangerous," was my instant reaction. "Here's a man I never saw before telling me I can take off my cast."

I turned to him to say, "You shouldn't do this to people," but when I looked him in the face, the words just wouldn't come out. He looked down at me and said again, "You can take off the cast if you want to."

The thought, "These people are dangerous," kept racing through my mind.

"Do you want to take off the cast?" he asked.

"I've been in this cast for 15 years and I'm dying," I answered. "Certainly I want to take it off."

He nodded his head for he, too, knew I was dying. The next thing I knew, he had me go into the women's room. Once there, I leaned against the wall and began ripping off my cast. Gail followed me into the women's room and asked, "What are you doing?"

"Taking my cast off," I replied.

"Why? Do you feel different?" she asked.

"No," I said.

Then she said, "Delores, this isn't like you."

So I started fastening my cast again. The man walked to the door of the women's room and said, "Come on. What are you waiting for?" I took another look at him and started ripping off my cast again. When it was completely off, I handed it to Gail and said, "Get me back out there to him."

Ready to Receive

The man and an usher helped me back into the auditorium. Just as they were sitting me down in my seat, Kathryn Kuhlman swung around and said, "What do you have there, Doctor?"

"I have a spine," said the man who had been helping me.

"Bring her here immediately!" she ordered.

"Uh-huh, he's a doctor," I mused. "That's why he knows what a percutaneous cordotomy is."

As the man she called "Doctor" and one of the ushers escorted me toward the stage, I thought, "Oh, dear God, I'm being put in the sideshow." I was relieved that no one in the audience knew me. Little did I know that before I would leave the stage that night, Kathryn Kuhlman would ask me to give my name and address to all 3,000 people assembled there.

When they finally got me up to Kathryn Kuhlman on the platform, she looked at me and said, "You're in a lot of pain, aren't you?"

"Yes," I replied, thinking that from the way I looked anyone could tell that I was in pain.

Then she ordered: "Walk to the back of the stage!"

The doctor said, "She can't, Kathryn; she doesn't have any support."

"Oh," she replied. "Doctor, tell the people what's wrong with her."

The doctor went to the microphone. He told the 3,000 people that surgeons had performed four spinal fusions and two percutaneous cordotomies on me. He explained that, although I could not feel anything in my legs, they were burning.

As the doctor was speaking, two other men held me in order to keep me from falling. Kathryn Kuhlman turned around, moved over to me, and repeated, "Now, walk to the back of the stage." Then she just stood there with her hands on her sides.

I thought, "She's not only weird, she didn't hear what the doctor told her about me." There I was without my cast or brace to support me. My body was all twisted. One of my legs was nearly an inch and a quarter shorter than the other. My spine was deteriorated. My body was bent over. Yet this woman was asking me to walk to the back of the stage. I was so weak, I couldn't even stand up by myself. Still, she said, "Walk."

AUGUST 2010 MEETING SCHEDULE

Sunday's: 5:30pm Fellowship Meal
MEETINGS START @ 7pm

<u>Sunday, August 1</u>: Pastor Mike Yeager, Cashtown, PA

<u>Wednesday, August 4</u>: Rev. Dr. Jerry Fitzgerald, Berwick, PA

<u>Saturday, August 7</u>: Jose Santana, Holley, NY **Prophetic Meeting for those Called To Be Pastors, Teachers, Leaders***

<u>Sunday, August 8:</u>   NO SERVICE

FELLOWSHIP MEAL @ 5:30 PM @ OAK GROVE FARMS, INC, 846 FISHER RD, MECHANICSBURG, PA

<u>Wednesday, August 11</u>: John McTernan, Liverpool, PA

<u>Saturday August 14</u> & <u>Sunday August 15</u>: Pastors Jim Law and Gary Shelton, Worship & the Word, Mechanicsburg, PA

<u>Wednesday, August 18</u>: Karen Roberts, Mechanicsburg, PA

<u>Saturday, August 21</u> & <u>Sunday August 22</u>: Joanna Coe Herndon, Waxahachie, TX

<u>Wednesday, August 25</u>: Dwayne Lebo, Mechanicsburg, PA

<u>Saturday August 28</u> & <u>Sunday August 29</u>: Harry Wingler, OH / Worship by Gary Shelton, Mechanicsburg, PA

I knew she was going to stand there looking at me, her hands on her sides, until I did something. I wondered if we were going to stand there the rest of the evening just looking at each other—in front of 3,000 people. I decided to push my right foot out to show her I couldn't walk.

When I put my foot out, it came up off the floor—the first time that had happened in years. And when my right foot came back down, I thought I could feel the floor. But an inner voice said, "No, you don't. You don't feel the floor."

All I knew for certain was that my foot had stepped out farther than I had expected or intended. A minister was holding me from the back; I knew that if he let go I would fall on my face, because I couldn't balance myself. I had to bring my left foot out because my right foot had stepped out farther than I had thought it would. When I put my left foot out, it came up off the floor and back down.

"I do feel the floor," I thought, but my mind kept saying, "No, you don't. You don't feel the floor. Get out of here. This is no place for you."

Then I felt my slacks rubbing against the tops of my legs. I started getting some feeling in my fingertips for the first time in the five years since the first cordotomy. I began to scream, "I can feel! I can feel!" But my screams of excitement didn't seem to mean a thing to Kathryn Kuhlman. She ordered me to walk to the back of the stage a third time. I honestly don't remember what happened after that.

Those who witnessed the miracle said that I took off running to the back of the stage. Then I ran back to Kathryn Kuhlman. I hadn't walked without help in five years, but there I was running around on the stage!

"Now, bend over," she said. My fusions were above my waist. I couldn't bend over; I hadn't been able to do so for years. The tissues in my back were shredding. My shoulder was so deteriorated that if I moved it, the agony was horrible. Yet she ordered me to bend over. Just to show her I could bend only a little, I started to bend over and suddenly realized that my shoulders were loose and moving. I kept bending until I touched the floor.

Actually, that was the first time in my life that I had ever touched the floor with my hands. The curvature in my spine had always been so bad that, even as a child, I couldn't bend over very far. But there I was, touching the floor—after having spine trouble and being in a brace or cast for 19½ years.

When I rose back up she said, "Do it again!" And I did, but this time I lay my hands flat on the floor and rose back up.

Then she ordered me to twist. "I can't do that because of the fusions," I thought. But deciding to try, I gingerly started twisting and found I had complete flexibility. By then the feeling was coming back into my whole body.

"Now, do you have any pain?" she asked me.

"No," I replied. I kept telling her that I could feel, but she seemed disinterested in that. Then it dawned on me—all the pain was gone!

Suddenly she reached out her hand to touch me. I grabbed the podium as visions of her knocking down those big, strong men danced through my mind. When they picked me up off the floor, I was still wondering what had happened. She looked at me again and said, "I think God would like for you to have a double dose." I fell to the floor again.

When I came out from under the influence of the Holy Spirit, she shook her finger at me and said, "That is the power of the Holy Spirit and don't you ever forget it! Now, you have work to do!" Those who witnessed the miracle that night said it took only 15 minutes for God to release me from all my chains of bondage and sickness.

I could never have imagined myself, a dying cripple who knew nothing of healing, leaving home at six o'clock in the evening and returning home completely healed by two o'clock the next morning. But, let me tell you, that's how God works. He does everything first class and He did so for me.

I later learned that the doctor who picked me out of the audience of 3,000 people was Dr. Richard Owellen of the Johns Hopkins Medical School in Baltimore, Maryland. He had become a faithful supporter of Kathryn Kuhlman's ministry following an event that took place in his family.

From time to time, a group of doctors traveled to wherever Kathryn Kuhlman was holding meetings. They did this to try to discredit her ministry. Dr. Owellen had been a member of that group; but after observing her ministry for a period of time, he became convinced that it was real. He became a faithful supporter of Miss Kuhlman's ministry.

Following one miraculous experience, Dr. Owellen received a gift from the Holy Spirit. It was the gift of knowledge. He began traveling to the various Kathryn Kuhlman meetings—no longer to discredit her ministry, but to help. Through the gift of knowledge, he often knew when someone in the audience was being healed. God would lead him directly to that person. That was what led him to me that night in Dallas.

On the morning of that Saturday when I was healed, Dr. Owellen had called one of Kathryn Kuhlman's aides in Dallas to inquire about the evening service. They informed him that the miracle services had been held Wednesday and Thursday nights at the Full Gospel Businessmen's conference. Then they told him that Saturday night's meeting was a Methodist conference on the Holy Spirit. Kathryn Kuhlman had been told she could speak on the Holy Spirit, but the conference leaders said they didn't want any healing ministry going on.

Dr. Owellen told them that he wouldn't be attending the Saturday night meeting because he had to fly to another city. Later, however, the Lord spoke to him and told him to go to Dallas. When he arrived, Kathryn Kuhlman's aides asked him, "What are you doing here?"

"The Lord sent me," he replied.

Dr. Owellen told me later that he had been sitting up on the platform during the early portion of the service. Then he got up, walked down one long aisle in the auditorium, then up another. He didn't stop walking until he got to me. I thought he had just picked me out of the crowd, but God had led him to me. And he got there just as I was trying to get away from the place.

Later I was told that I probably would not have received my healing had it not been for Dr. Owellen. If I had left that meeting, believing as I did that God no longer healed people and thinking my legs were burning because of the cast rubbing against them, I might never have been healed. I would have left that auditorium still dying and burdened with all the other diseases in which satan had trapped me. Instead, I walked off that stage completely healed. Praise be to God!

Coming Home Whole

After the service concluded, the people were praising God. Several people wished me well and said they would be praying for me. They were all greatly excited over my healing.

As we prepared to say good-bye that night, Dr. Owellen said, "Delores, I have to caution you about something. Satan is going to try to tell you that you've not been healed." I backed away from the doctor.

I didn't talk about satan. Satan didn't bother my family or me. He lived in hell.

I told them good-bye and Gail and I left the auditorium. We walked to the car, carrying the cast and neck brace. I threw the cast in the back seat with the pillows and blankets, opened the front door of the car, and very spryly stepped inside. Gail hadn't said a word; she was still as white as a sheet. She broke the silence by saying, "What are you going to tell Bill?"

"I don't know," I replied. She was driving only about five miles per hour; in her mind she was figuring out that I had a problem ahead.

"Please put your cast on," she implored me.

"No! I feel great!" I told her.

Surges of energy and strength were just coursing through me. The strength would go up and down my body. Each time it made a full circuit, I became stronger.

Can you imagine what it was like for Gail—who had cared for me all those years—to see me made completely whole? Or can you imagine what it would be like for Bill and Chris to see me come home a new person? In their worry and concern, they kept looking out the front window, waiting for Gail to bring me home.

When we arrived back at Gail's house, she pulled into her driveway and abruptly said, "I'll see you tomorrow." Then she jumped out of the car and started toward her house.

"Oh, no! What am I going to tell Bill?" I called to her.

"I can't help you. Good night," she said.

Chris had seen us pull into Gail's driveway. He bolted out of our house and stood across the street waiting for me. As I stepped out of the car he came running across the street screaming, "Mother, you were healed! You were healed!"

That Sunday morning, August 31, 1975, at 2 A.M., was the first time in his 14 years that Chris had ever seen me get out of a car by myself. Still screaming, he picked me up and swung me round and round.

He had always had to touch me gently. But now he was swinging me around in the middle of the street and yelling his lungs out at two o'clock in the morning. Then he picked me up and started carrying me toward our house. Bill stepped out on the front porch.

When he saw Chris carrying me, Bill went back into the house.

Chris was still screaming. I tried to quiet him down, saying he would awaken the neighbors. Chris didn't care. He just kept screaming and shouting until he got me to the house. The first question Chris asked me was: "Mother, can we go to church together tomorrow, our whole family?"

"Sure we can," I answered.

When we walked into the house, Bill looked at me rather skeptically for a minute and asked, "Where's your cast?"

"In the car," I replied. Seeing the shock on his face, I said, "Bill, I'm all right. Look." I began moving my head to show him my neck was free. Then I bent over and touched my hands to the floor.

"And I can feel!" I said gleefully, clenching my fists open and shut. Staring at me in disbelief Bill said, "OK, you can feel. Now let's go to bed."

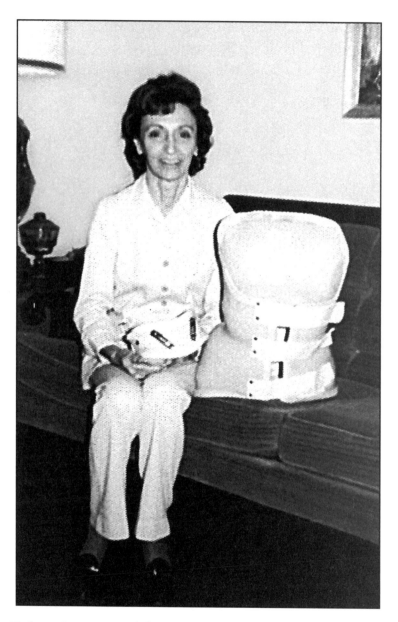

Delores in 1975 with her brace, which she no longer needed, after God healed her at a Kathryn Kuhlman conference.

For the first time in 11 years, I went to bed without taking any pills. I fell into a deep sleep and slept like a baby all night. Bill never went to bed that night.

To some people that might have been the beautiful ending of a sad story; but it wasn't.

It was the beginning of a nightmare for Bill and me.

Chapter 5

Good Times, Bad Times

So if the Son sets you free,
you will be free indeed
(John 8:36).

I woke up at seven o'clock the next morning and felt great! I went to the bathroom to take a shower by myself for the first time in seven years. The first thing I did when I got to the bathroom was tear the bandage off my back. There had been an open, draining sore on my back for seven months. I got into the shower and gave my 73-pound body the scrubbing of its life.

After drying off with a towel all by myself, I went out to the kitchen. Bill heard me and came into the kitchen from the den.

He just stared at me and asked, "What are you doing?"

"I'm going to eat something. Then we're going to church," I replied.

"Hmm," he muttered. Bill said nothing more.

Chris was jumping up and down because we were going to church. "Do you really feel like going to church?" Bill finally asked.

"Yes, Bill, I feel great!" I told him.

"OK, we'll go," he said. Bill went to the bedroom and started dressing for church.

When I walked into the bedroom, he said, "Let's dress the sore on your back."

"All right," I said.

He assembled the necessary bandages but, when I turned around for him to apply them, Bill said, "The sore has scarred over." I swung around and looked at him. He was as stunned as I was.

I turned around so I could see my back in the mirror. The sore was indeed gone. All that remained was a small, white scar. It looked like an old scar except it appeared as if someone had taken a pin and drawn out blood in a circle around the scar, making a red ring around it. Bill just sighed and went back to the bedroom.

Suddenly, I realized that we were now living out something that neither of us understood. Overnight, I had been transformed from a hopeless invalid to a perfectly well, energetic woman. Who could possibly understand it?

I was so free and jubilant. Just to see the joy in Chris's face caused great happiness to well up within me. Bill, however, was silent as we drove toward the Presbyterian Church. Bill later told me he had made up his mind that, if whatever happened to me lasted even one or two days, it would be worth it. Whatever the outcome, we would try to be happy.

My husband was a structural steel inspector, but he had minored in psychology in college. Bill's psychology background kept indicating to him that this couldn't be happening; it had to be some kind of illusion.

Again, he decided that, even if I had been hypnotized (or whatever!), he would accept it for as long as it lasted. If I were to subsequently collapse, he would just deal with it.

We walked into church and discovered that the pastor was out of town. No one there that day recognized me. I had purposed in my heart that I would tell no one about my healing until I had a chance to discuss it with Van, my doctor.

As we walked out of church that day I said to Bill, "Let's go to the Colonial Cafeteria and eat."

He turned to me and said, "You sure you feel up to it?"

"I feel great and I'm starved!" I told him.

"I think you had better go home and rest," he said. Of course, there was no way Bill could understand my sudden hunger, because for years I had no appetite.

Surges of energy kept flooding through my body. It would enter through the soles of my feet and rise to my head. Then the process would be repeated, my body growing stronger each time. By the following Sunday, I knew I could take on the whole world!

The food in the cafeteria line looked so good to me. By the time we had gone through the line, there was enough food on my tray to feed the whole family. I ate cucumbers in vinegar, fried chicken, watermelon, and cherry pie. Bill just sat and watched.

While sitting there in the cafeteria, it finally dawned on me that my years of sickness were over. God really had healed me! However, my dear, wonderful Bill kept searching for some rational explanation for what had happened. Of course, there was no natural explanation, only a supernatural one. It was just going to take him a while to understand it all.

The Shock of a New Reality

That afternoon, we decided to drive over to Mansfield, Texas, to see our 30-year-old son Doug, his wife Ann, and our grandchildren. That was the day I made my first mistake after being healed.

When we drove up to their home, Doug was working in the yard. He saw our car, but of course, knew I was too sick to make the trip to Mansfield. So Doug presumed I was at home. I slipped out of the car and walked over to where he was working. When he looked around and saw me, it startled him.

"Mother, what are you doing here?" he asked. I hadn't been to his home in 18 months.

I looked at him, smiled, and said, "Could you use me on your football team?" I thought he would appreciate me saying that because Doug is a coach. Then I bent over in front of him and placed the palms of my hands squarely on the ground. When I rose up, I knew I shouldn't have approached him that way.

Unexpectedly, Doug couldn't get his breath. I thought he was having a heart attack right there in his front yard. He began shaking as if he had chills. Bill grabbed him and helped him into the house where he sat down.

Ann, our daughter-in-law, had come outside just in time to see me touch the ground with the palms of my hands. She began screaming and said, "Mother, what are you doing?"

"It's all right, Ann, I'm healed."

Ann was trembling. "What do you mean you are healed?" she asked.

"I don't know, but I'm healed. I'm all right now," I told her.

During the final stages of my illness, Ann would often come to our home in Arlington to dress the sore on my back for me. Naturally she wanted to know if the sore was still there. "Mother, let me see the sore," she said. When I showed her the sore, she exclaimed, "It's healed! What happened?"

I couldn't explain anything to them because I didn't understand it myself. I didn't know anyone could be healed or ever was healed. I had never even talked to anyone who knew a person who had been healed. All I could say to Doug and Ann was, "Look, I'm standing here. I feel fine. All the feeling is back in my body."

Doug, still pale and unable to stand the trauma any longer, said, "Mother, I think you had better go home. I'm going to have to take some time to work through this." So we went home. The nightmare had begun.

The Fight to Keep the Victory

God healed me during Labor Day weekend when Bill had a couple of days off from work. When he went back to work and left me alone in the house, I learned that I was completely unprepared to be by myself. Crazy thoughts started running through my mind. "I'm still not well," I thought. "My mind is just gone."

I would go stand in front of a large mirror, look at myself, and say, "No, I'm healed! Look, I can move my head and bend and lift my feet. And I can walk." My mind needed a lot of convincing to understand what had happened to my body.

One thing that complicated our understanding of the miracle was that neither Bill nor I had ever received any teaching on healing. We had never read a book or heard a sermon on the subject. When we ran across verses on healing while reading God's Word, we didn't understand their meaning.

I cried more during the first ten days after my healing than during my entire 19½ years of illness. After the difficult experience with Doug and Ann, I was afraid to tell anyone what had happened.

On Monday night, I had an attack on my herniated esophagus. It startled me out of a deep sleep. Immediately I grabbed for a bottle of pain pills. A still, quiet voice inside me said, "Don't take the pills." I put them back on the shelf.

I knew I had to do something. The pain in my esophagus was intense. Sweat was pouring off my body like water. "What can I do?" I cried out. Again, the quiet voice spoke to me and said, "Get up."

That was strange. Usually when I had such attacks, I would pass out cold if I tried to get up. Then Bill would have to take me to the hospital cardiac care unit.

The voice again said, "Get up. Now."

"I can't get up," I argued. A third time the voice said, "Get up." As I began to get up out of bed, I said, "If I pass out, it's not my fault." Sitting on the edge of the bed, I looked at the clock. It was 11 P.M.

I stood and walked to the bathroom and sat down again, all knotted up, shaking from pain and fear. "I won't have this!" I shouted, and then I started getting angry. "God, I won't have this!" I screamed.

Suddenly, it felt as though something opened up inside of my chest and then came out of it. The pressure and pain disappeared. I dried off with a towel and returned to bed, weak and drained. As I sat down on the bed I noticed the clock again. It was 11:10 P.M. The attack lasted only ten minutes. It had seemed like hours.

Dr. Richard Casdorph, a Spirit-filled physician, later asked me if I understood what had happened during the esophagus attack. I told him I did not understand it at all.

He said I had engaged in spiritual warfare. Satan had tried to put the illness back on me, he explained. He added that God would not always protect me as He had done that night. I would have to learn for myself how to combat the evil one, using all the spiritual provisions God had made for me.

God placed a covering over me for about a year; then He stepped back. But I learned to take authority over pain in the name of Jesus. When I prayed, the pain always went away.

Everything was so unreal and frightening. Bill and I didn't even discuss what had happened to me. We were sort of pretending that it hadn't happened. Bill just went along accepting my improvement, even though he really didn't think it would last.

On Tuesday night when I stepped out of the shower, Bill saw my back and his face lit up as he realized it was no longer twisted. I had been twisted and bent, with one leg shorter than the other. For the first time in our married life he observed that my shoulders and hips were even. "Something did happen to you," he admitted, shaking his head, still unable to logically understand the phenomenon.

It was also on Tuesday that I had to deal with strange words going around in my mind. The words had appeared when I first awakened on Sunday morning. I knew they weren't Latin or French, but that was all I understood about them.

Satan kept telling me that I had lost my mind and gone bananas. Then he started whispering in my ear, telling me the strange words were proof I was going crazy. At that time I didn't even believe that satan existed, except as the keeper of the pit in hell. Nevertheless, he kept whispering, "Well, it really happened. You've lost your mind."

Through the years, one of my greatest fears was that I would lose my mind before I died. I was a ripe candidate for insanity. I had taken so many drugs, had so much surgery, and had suffered so much pain that my mind had become dull. I couldn't remember things that happened from one hour to the next.

The night I was healed God completely delivered me from the drug habit which had worried me. I had been led to believe that no one went off drugs without enduring the pains of withdrawal. Yet I had. Still, the fear of losing my mind provided satan with an opening to hit me where I was weak. He'll take that opportunity every time.

My emotions swung from confidence to fear. I would stand in front of the mirror, bend over, touch the floor, and then cry out, "I am healed! I don't understand it, but I am healed!" But by the time I walked halfway down the hall of the house, I was convinced once again that I was crazy.

A Professional Witness

On Wednesday Bill called Van, my doctor, and told him we wanted to see him. He told us to come on by his office. We went into the waiting room, where I sat down. That in itself was unusual; ordinarily I would have been lying down on the sofa while waiting for my appointment.

As soon as Van walked into the waiting room he looked at me and said, "You're different. What happened?"

"Van, I want you to check me thoroughly," I said.

"Your neck, your back, your shoulder, or what?" he asked.

"Everything," I answered.

"Well, all right," he said, a puzzled look on his face.

"Just check me, Van," I said.

"OK," he replied.

He helped me move into his examination room, just as he always had. Then he said, "You're moving awfully well."

I really wasn't trying to move; I wanted Van to help move me. Before I had left the auditorium the night of my healing, Dr. Owellen had told me, "Have your doctor check you, but don't tell him what happened until after he is through with the examination."

Van stood me up and said, "Hold her," to his nurse. He and the nurse both were careful not to touch my left shoulder because the x-rays had shown that it was deteriorating. While examining me, he began to bend me over a little and then stopped.

As I rose up and turned toward him, I saw that he was almost in a daze sitting on the edge of his stool. He looked at me and said, "Let me see your sore." He knew that the sore had been draining for several months. He took one look at where the sore had been and said, "It's healed. What has happened to you?"

"No, Van, I want you to go on checking me—everything," I said, not answering his question.

"OK," he said, almost reluctantly. He wanted to place me on an examination table and started to help me get on it.

"I can do it by myself, Van," I told him.

I climbed up on the table with ease. Van started to turn me over and I said, "I can turn over." And I did. He began touching my spine, pressing on my neck lightly at first and then harder.

"That isn't hurting you?" he asked.

"No," I said.

Then he ran both hands up and down my spine. "Your spine is straight," he said, in utter disbelief. "Delores, tell me what happened."

"Finish the examination first," I said.

He reached over and touched my shoulder. Van had not done that in two years because a simple touch in that area would have resulted in excruciating pain. As he inched his hand toward my shoulder, he watched to see if I would pull away from him as before. "I haven't touched your shoulder in two-and-a-half years," he said.

"Van, give me your hand," I told him, reaching toward him. I took his hand and squeezed it. By that time, my grip was like steel.

"What happened to you?" he asked again.

"We're not finished," I replied.

"I guess you want me to use the pin, too?" he asked.

"Yes," I said.

"Then lay back down and don't look," he instructed.

He took a pin and stuck my legs, arms, and stomach—all the places where I'd had no feeling for years, but only numbness due to the cordotomies. Unable to endure the curiosity any longer, he said, "OK, that's it. Tell me what happened. But let me sit down first." He pulled a stool over by the examination table and sat down.

I told him what had happened—all of it. The doctor sat with his head down as I related the story of my miraculous healing.

Tears streamed from his eyes. "Now, Van, you tell me how this could have happened," I said.

In the back of my mind, for some unknown reason, I kept hoping there was some medical explanation for what had happened to me. I was seeking a way out, for it was all just too much for my mind to comprehend. I hoped he would say, "Look, Delores, this is what really happened," then give me a rational explanation.

To my great dismay, he looked at me and said, "Delores, this is truly a miracle—there is no other way." Then he added, "You have work to do for the Lord." Those words made me uneasy as I remembered that Kathryn Kuhlman had told me virtually the same thing the night I was healed. Van was still shocked when Bill and I left his office and went home.

Signs of New Life

Van wasn't the only one who was amazed. One day while at work, Bill was laughing and joking, just having a good time with some of the other men. His joyful attitude caused his friend Lee to ask him, "Why are you so happy?" Lee knew of my illness and had understood that I was dying. He was just amazed that Bill was so happy.

"My wife was healed!" Bill replied.

"Really! That's great!" Lee exclaimed, a broad grin spreading across his face.

"Do you believe that?" Bill asked, astonished at Lee's interest.

"Well, of course," Lee said. "Do you think your wife would come to our church and give her testimony?"

Bill took Lee's words very seriously. When he told me about the conversation, I asked, "Bill, you told him no, didn't you?"

"No," he replied.

"Bill, you know I won't do that!" I shouted. He didn't answer.

After letting me cool down a little, Bill again asked, "What should I tell Lee about your visiting his church to tell the people what happened to you?"

After pondering the question for some time, and with an inner urging impressing me to accept the invitation, I reluctantly agreed to go. "OK, just this one time, but don't ever ask me to do it again," I said.

But it didn't end there. That Thursday, a beautiful woman who had been in and out of our home for years walked into the house. When she entered the dining room where I was sitting, I looked at her. Suddenly, it was as though the pages of a pornographic book were turning and I was reading the story of her life.

Immediately I knew she was a lesbian and was in the midst of an affair with another woman. "Oh, dear God, I'd rather be dead than to see things like this," I thought. It was frightening, even sickening. I saw scenes of her activity and suddenly it was over. But I saw it; it was hard and sinful and sick.

There was nothing I knew to do to help her, so we just had a visit and then she left. After that I quit answering the telephone. I didn't want anyone else to come to my house and see the seemingly crazy woman I had become. I didn't understand what God was doing at the time.

The experience was just another episode convincing me that I had perhaps lost my mind. Maggie Hartner, a close associate of Kathryn Kuhlman's, then started calling me every day, but I couldn't even tell her what was happening.

The people at our church did not understand healing. They had never received any teaching on the subject, and it was not spoken of publicly in the church. Therefore, my healing was rejected by the people, and that hurt.

There was a woman in the church who had been very good to visit me during the last stages of my illness. One day she called and asked if we could have lunch together. I said, "Yes, I would love it."

We went to a restaurant and there she related an incredible story to me that made me weep. "Delores, I know what you are going through," she began.

"What do you mean?" I asked.

"I know about how the people have rejected you and how you feel." Then she added, "I want to tell you a story." She related to me one of the saddest stories I've ever heard.

"I was a mental patient in an institution after the birth of my child," she said. "The doctors told my husband that I would never get out. I was too sick. But there in the mental hospital, Jesus appeared to me and healed me. A short time later I was released." Her face was saddened as she continued the story. "But the people in the church would have nothing to do with me," she said. "So we had to move away. We moved here where no one knew the story. That's how I know what you're going through."

She said the rejection from the people in her church almost broke her down again, causing her to be on the verge of having to return to the mental institution. "But God held onto me. We moved. Nobody here knows anything about it," she said, sighing. After hearing that story from this dear woman, I better understood the rejection I was receiving from the people at my church.

The next Sunday, we drove to the little Foursquare church in Dallas where I was to give my testimony. Lee greeted us and seemed so very excited that we were there.

I was not prepared for what I experienced that morning in the Foursquare church! God really treated me roughly, probably because I was being so hard-headed about my healing. I still wanted to use reason and logic to describe and understand what had happened to me.

As we were sitting there in the Foursquare church, a woman named Brenda came into the service. A little later the pastor announced that Brenda would sing. She walked to the platform carrying a tape recorder and said, "I heard a new song this week and just love it. I want to sing it for you today." The song was about God's healing power.

At that time, I didn't realize just how skeptical I was about everything. When Brenda began to sing about healing, I thought sarcastically, "Boy, this is really a build-up." My heart was full of resentment.

After Brenda sang, the pastor walked to the pulpit and introduced me to the congregation. As I walked toward the platform, Brenda stood and gave a prophecy. It was the first one I had ever heard.

The prophecy was given in "tongues," but I heard it in perfect English. I didn't know the utterance was in tongues. What I heard made me mad and frightened. She had the audacity to go into my life for the next 20 years. There I was, holding on to the pulpit, getting madder every minute. The woman was prophesying about how God was going to use me in His work.

"Why is she saying that stuff?" I asked myself, fuming inside. "That's not true! I'm not going to do that! And all these people are hearing it!"

Brenda completed the prophecy. Then I struggled through the testimony of my healing, going into detail about all that had happened.

After it was over, I really "lost it." The minister's wife came up to me, grabbed hold of me, and said, "Oh, I need a touch from God and just want to hold you."

"Don't hold on to me!" I told her rudely as I backed away from her in disgust. "I don't have anything for you." I was furious when we left the church that morning. The experience at the Foursquare church really knocked the props out from under me. I was finished!

While driving back to Arlington, Bill said, "The testimony was fine." I really didn't remember what I had said. All I remembered was the repulsion of having to do it. It must have been all right, though; the minister (who was a sweet man) invited me to come back and speak at the church again—even after the way I treated his wife.

As we drove toward home I became madder and madder. Finally, I broke the silence and said, "Bill, don't ever ask me to do that again! That's it! You've had it! I don't ever want to hear about it again!"

Chris just sat quietly in the back seat, listening intently. "Why? What's wrong?" he asked.

"What that woman Brenda said! Why did she stand there and say all of that stuff? She doesn't even know me!"

"What did she say?" Bill asked. Then I really got mad.

"What do you mean, what did she say?" I scolded.

Then it dawned on me that neither Bill nor Chris had understood what Brenda had said, because she was speaking in tongues. But why did I understand it, every word of it? Having no teaching or experience with tongues, I again thought I was losing my mind. I began to cry.

After we arrived home, I called the pastor of the Foursquare church and asked him if he had understood Brenda's prophecy. He said he hadn't, but he sensed that it was a personal prophecy for me. He thought perhaps the Lord was laying out my ministry.

All of this was too much for me; I had to walk away from it. Maggie Hartner, Kathryn's associate, called the next day. I told her about the experience with the pastor's wife and her wanting to hold me in order to get a touch from the Lord. I told her about the prophecy. Maggie told me she would discuss it with Kathryn. Then she added, "I feel like you shouldn't have been so curt with that woman."

Kathryn Kuhlman told Maggie to tell me to point people to Jesus by saying, "You can't plug into me. You must plug into Jesus." That was really good advice.

Not Crazy, but Baptized!

Complicating all the other personal problems I was having, my phone just rang off the hook. Kathryn Kuhlman had me give my name and address to all 3,000 people present the night I was healed. Many of them called to ask if my healing was real and whether it had lasted. They wanted to know how I was feeling and asked lots of other bothersome questions.

During those days, satan tried to take my mind. I would stand in front of the mirror and look at myself. I looked OK, but something kept telling me it was only an illusion caused by all the medication I had taken during my illness.

I was convinced I had lost my mind. One of the great fears I carried during my illness was that the painkillers and tranquilizers would destroy my mind. Satan convinced me that it had happened.

I stopped answering the phone because I felt I could no longer tell people I was healed.

Then God sent Velma Despain back into my life. She just popped in and asked, "Would you like to go for a ride?"

"Yes," I replied, "I'll do anything to get out of this house and away from that phone."

Velma took me for a ride all right, right up to an Assembly of God preacher. He invited us into his study. "Velma said I should meet you. I've been trying to reach you but couldn't, so I just asked God to send you to me."

I was embarrassed to tell him I hadn't been answering the phone. I wanted to run and hide, but decided to stay and listen to him.

"You were baptized when you were healed, weren't you?" he asked.

"No, I was baptized in the Methodist church when I was a child," I replied.

Then he realized that I didn't understand what he was talking about.

It really blew my mind when he said that God had revealed to him what had happened to me, even though he had never seen me in my whole life. And I thought, "He's as crazy as I am."

Then he began asking me questions, and I knew I was crazy.

He asked, "Are you saying strange words?"

"No," I replied.

"Do you know some things you think you shouldn't know?" he probed.

That question stumped me; I couldn't answer.

"You're not saying strange words?" he continued.

"No," I stubbornly replied.

"Do you have strange words running around in your head?" he asked.

Then I started to cry. "Do you know what happened to you?" he asked.

"Yes, I've lost my mind," I said, weeping profusely.

"No, you haven't," the gentle minister assured me. "You were baptized in the Holy Spirit when you were healed and you received some gifts." As I got control of myself again, I continued to listen.

"Do you know about the Holy Spirit?" he asked.

"No," I replied.

The minister took his Bible and began to teach me. He read where Jesus told the disciples that He is the baptizer in the Holy Spirit. He then read where Jesus told His disciples to wait until the Holy Spirit came upon them. Obediently they waited until the power of the Holy Spirit fell at Pentecost. Then Peter, empowered by the Holy Spirit, began witnessing and preaching to the Romans without concern for his personal safety because of the boldness he had received when the Holy Spirit came upon him.

That kind, patient minister also taught me about the gifts and the fruit of the Spirit.

"But all that isn't for today. That doesn't happen anymore," I said.

"What do you think happened to you?" he gently asked. "How did you get healed if not by the miraculous power of God?"

Still struggling with my worldview, I repeated, "This is not valid for today. Healing ceased after the apostolic age."

"No, Delores, the Bible doesn't teach that. Man says that, not God," the pastor told me. "Can you show me in God's Word where He recalls the Holy Spirit or revokes the gifts of the Spirit?"

"No, I can't," was my reply.

"No, because He never did," he said. Then he asked me if I had any questions.

"Will I always know bad things about people?" I asked.

"No, not unless God is going to use you to set them free or to help them through it," he answered.

Ever so slowly, my spiritual eyes began to open. I realized I wasn't going crazy; God had baptized me in the Holy Spirit.

As Velma and I drove back to my home, things looked a lot brighter. There were still some unanswered questions in my mind, but God was putting the pieces of that giant jigsaw puzzle together.

A short time later, the woman God revealed to me to be a lesbian came to visit me again. For some reason unknown to me, she began telling me her story, just as I had seen it in the Spirit.

As she related the story, a strange thing happened. It was as though God was writing on my hand four things she had to do to be set free. I looked at the four things. They were so simple that I was convinced they wouldn't work. "I know this won't work, but there are four things that I see you should do," I told her. Then I shared them with her.

Number one was to truly repent and ask God to forgive her. As soon as I completed the four things God asked her to do, I immediately forgot the last three and don't remember them to this day. Those three were only for her. That day the woman got down on her knees in my living room and truly repented.

After she left, satan began kicking me all over the place. "Boy, you really made a fool out of yourself," he said to me. "How did you think you could help her? That's her life and you're meddling in it. What do you think you're doing? You think you're so smart." I felt terrible.

But two months later the woman came back to our home. She walked in and the first thing she said was, "I'm free! I did it and I'm free."

Amazement swept over me. How could this be? It's another miracle! Years later, she is *still* free. There is no thought of her former sin. She has thanksgiving in her heart because Jesus set her free.

Chapter 6

THE SURRENDER

But seek first His kingdom and His righteousness,
and all these things will be given to you as well
(Matthew 6:33).

"Praise God, that first year after my healing was horrible!"
I fought Bill; he fought me. Bill insisted that I accept
the invitations I had received to speak in churches. I
insisted that I stay home, plant flowers, and take care of my family,
something I had been deprived of doing for 19½ years. There was a constant battle around our house. It lasted for weeks…even months.

The problem was that Delores Winder was in the driver's seat, not
God. Nothing works very well when we get those positions reversed.

Following my healing, Bill had started spending long hours reading
God's Word. Through the months, he was saved, baptized in the Holy
Spirit, and became much more spiritually perceptive and obedient than
I was.

I even tried to tell God what to do. Can you imagine that? After
accepting an invitation to speak in a church I would say, "All right, God.
I'll go and tell them what happened to me, but don't heal anyone."

79

Then things got pretty neat. A few days after the service, people would write to say they had been healed while I was speaking. I would say, "OK, God, I accept that. You can do that." I was totally filled with rebellion. Can you imagine me, of all people, telling God what He could and could not do—and how He could do it?

On-the-Road Testimonies

A couple of weeks after my healing, I received a call from Maggie. She said Kathryn wanted me to go to Oklahoma City to give my testimony during a meeting there. She also asked me to bring my cast and neck brace. I told Maggie to give me time to think about it.

Bill and Chris both wanted to go. Bill knew immediately why I had been invited. But I was so dumb, so naive. I really couldn't imagine why they invited me and particularly why they wanted me to bring the cast and neck brace, those symbols of so much pain and suffering in my life. Finally, I consented.

When we arrived at the auditorium in Oklahoma City where Kathryn Kuhlman was to minister, we met several people who had been in Dallas the night I was healed. I tried to shove my cast and neck brace off on them. I didn't want to be seen with the things. They would say, "Just hold on to them."

The service began and there was singing and special music by Jimmy McDonald. Bill, Chris, and I sat in the large auditorium enjoying the music.

Kathryn came out on stage with her usual flair, saying grandly, "I believe in miracles!" She spoke for a while, then abruptly turned to Jimmy McDonald and said, "Jimmy, a couple of weeks ago in Dallas we saw a woman healed, and you just stood there and cried. I want you to see that woman today." Then Donnie, one of her staff members, walked over toward me. Suddenly, I realized why she had invited me to the meeting.

There we were in a large, packed auditorium and Kathryn Kuhlman was asking me to stand up in front of all that crowd and tell what had happened to me in Dallas. The crowd didn't scare me. I just wanted to be left alone so I could live my own life, adjust to my healing, and go about my business.

I grabbed Bill's arm. He took my hand and placed it back in my lap. Bill was turning me loose and wasn't going to protect me. That was disappointing to me. I was in total rebellion, so the Lord worked through Bill. When Donnie got to where we were sitting, I took the cast and neck brace and shoved them at him.

"No, she wants you," Donnie said calmly.

"I'm not going," I said.

Kathryn looked over at us, grinned, and said, "She doesn't want to have any part of me. She doesn't like me." The audience broke into laughter. Kathryn laughed too. She was laughing because she had seen so many others who had been healed in her meetings act the same way.

Suddenly I said to myself, "OK, I'll show her!" I stood up and walked to the front of the auditorium and up on stage.

"Tell the people what happened to you," Kathryn ordered in her own inimitable, persuasive way. Then she planted her hand on my back; I was so close to the microphone that I couldn't move.

I told the people about my healing in Dallas. After my testimony was concluded, Kathryn ordered me to bend over. I bent over and touched my toes, even though I was wearing high-heeled shoes that night for the first time in many years.

Then Kathryn asked, "Is everything all right now?"

The rebellion rose up inside me and I replied, "I still have a numb hand and there is burning around my back."

"Let's just see what the Lord will do about that tonight," Kathryn said. When she touched me, I fell to the floor.

I'm not sure how long I lay there, but when I woke up the numbness in my hand and burning in my back were completely gone.

Later, I realized that the burning in my back was around the area where they had tried several times to fuse new bone into my vertebrae. Now the pain was completely gone, never to return.

As we drove home that night, I was all torn up inside. I determined in my heart that I would never again speak before a crowd like that or go near Kathryn Kuhlman.

The next week, I received another call from Maggie Hartner asking me to go to California to make a videotape of my testimony with Kathryn. "There's no way I'm going to do it," I told Maggie. "I never want to be around that woman again!"

Then I started having muscle spasms in my back. Bill told me to go to California.

"No. I won't go!" I yelled at him.

"Yes, you will go. You owe them that much," he said.

"I don't owe them a thing," I replied.

"You *will* go," Bill said.

"I can't go and say, 'I'm healed,' when I'm having bad spasms in my back," I said, trying to justify my rebellion.

Bill kept bugging me by saying, "You're going to get rid of those muscle spasms the very minute you decide to go to California."

Finally, I gave up and decided to go. I wrote Maggie a letter and told her I would rather wait and go to California in November, instead of in October as Kathryn had wanted. I was trying to buy some time.

When I dropped the letter into the mailbox I breathed a prayer, "Lord, help them to forget all about me." As soon as I mailed the letter, the muscle spasms stopped, just as Bill had predicted.

I felt caught in a trap. Every time I tried to run away, the trap would snap shut. It was a horrible feeling. It hadn't dawned on me that God was dealing with me through Kathryn Kuhlman; but He was. He had to use someone He could trust. That someone sure wasn't me.

God kept urging me to do things, and I kept putting them off. Each afternoon, when it was time for Bill to return home from work, I would get upset. I was convinced he could read my mind. He was always telling me things I should do, things that already were on my mind. I would think to myself, "I've got to get rid of this thought before Bill gets here."

When Bill would come in the door, he would say, "You know, there's something I think you need to do." I would cringe inside. My husband was hearing things from the Lord and being obedient. I was hearing those same things and trying to run away from them. It was a confused, mixed-up period in our lives.

The time came for me to go to California. Maggie told me that in addition to making the videotape with Kathryn, she also wanted me to appear with Kathryn at a service in the Shrine Auditorium in Los Angeles.

For the first time in 20 years, I found myself on an airplane and, after that, alone in a hotel room. After arriving at the hotel I felt pretty good. Bill wasn't there "reading my mind," and I could close the door and keep everyone out.

The next morning, they came to take me to the CBS studio for the taping. I knew that meant sitting around listening to Kathryn Kuhlman's staff talking about demons, evil spirits, deliverance, and healing—things I wasn't eager to hear about.

The following morning an aide called and asked me to go to the studio again.

"Why must I go to the studio?" I asked. "I'll not be taping until the last day."

"Because Kathryn wants you there," the aide replied.

"Well, who is Kathryn, anyway?" I asked, sarcastically. The whole thing chafed against my old nature and brought out my rough edges.

Something very unusual happened after we finished taping. The CBS camera crew, the same crew that worked for Sonny and Cher, came over and wanted to talk about my healing. They asked me all kinds of questions. "That's the first time the crew has ever wanted to talk to anyone on my program," Kathryn told me later.

I decided to go to San Diego after the taping to see Winnie and Verne, two of my dearest friends. I called Winnie the night before and told her I planned to visit them. Only two months earlier they had visited me in Arlington and saw me dying.

"Where are you? Are you in a hospital?" Winnie asked.

"I'm in Los Angeles," I replied.

"Are you in a hospital?" she asked again.

"No, I'm coming to see you," I said.

"Who's coming with you?" she asked.

"Winnie, I'll see you tomorrow," I said.

Winnie later told me that after she hung up the phone she told Verne, "Delores is in Los Angeles in a hospital. They've found some way to help her."

Before I arrived in San Diego it hadn't dawned on me that I would have to walk down the ramp at the airport. Winnie was expecting to see someone helping me down the steps from the airplane.

When she and Verne saw me walking by myself, Verne almost collapsed. I walked into the passenger's lounge to see him sitting in a chair, chalk white and shaking like a leaf. He kept saying, "Oh, my God! Oh, my God! What has happened?"

Of course, they had heard nothing about my healing and wanted to know all about it.

The visit with Winnie and Verne was enjoyable, but it was good to get back home to Bill and Chris. Chris had changed so much in the short time following my healing that I had to be thankful, for him, that I was still alive—even though I wasn't thankful for myself.

Two Hearts Healed

People continued to invite me to speak at various meetings. As usual, I told God I didn't want people to be healed during the services. I told Him I would appreciate it if He would just heal them after it was all over and I could hear about it later.

Somehow the devil had me convinced that open manifestations of healing bordered on being a sideshow and I didn't want to picture myself as a "sideshow faith healer." But one night God said, "No more of this. No more."

People increasingly began being healed during the meetings, and there was nothing I could do about it. But it took nearly two years before I could accept God's using me as a vessel of His healing power.

One night, I was invited to minister to a group of people at Barksdale Air Force Base in Bossier City, Louisiana. During the service the Lord revealed to me that He was healing a heart condition.

Out of obedience to God, I invited the person with the heart condition to lift a hand and receive the healing. No one moved, but in my spirit I knew, for certain, that a heart was being healed. Then I saw a little boy standing in a chair with both of his hands in the air, but I ignored him.

I repeated, "I know the heart healing is here tonight."

The reason I was so certain of a heart condition in the audience was that my own heart was behaving like the heart that needed to be healed. My heartbeat became very irregular, stopping and then starting again. As I continued to ask someone to claim the healing of the heart, the little boy's mother placed her hand on his chest to check his heartbeat.

When my own heart became normal again, I told the audience, "The heart is beating in a regular pattern now. Please claim it." No one moved. "Dear God, why doesn't someone accept it?" I prayed. But no one did.

After the service the little boy's mother brought him up to me. His name was Eric. His mother said he had been healed. She had placed her hand on his chest and felt his heart beating just as I had described it.

Then Eric's mother told me a heartwarming story about her son. She explained that Eric was an orphan. No one would adopt him until he was a year old because of his heart condition. The people at the adoption agency told prospective parents that Eric would have to have heart surgery when he was five years old. They also explained that he had only a 30 percent chance of survival.

Even though Eric had a bad heart, this woman and her husband were willing to take him in as their own. He was scheduled for open-heart surgery the next week.

I looked at the little five-year-old boy and asked, "Do you want to thank Jesus for healing you?"

He said, "Yes."

I prayed a simple prayer asking God to put the assurance in Eric's heart that he truly had been healed. After the prayer, Eric looked at me with his sparkling, chocolate-brown eyes and said, "Don't ever stop praying." His words broke my heart.

Suddenly, my own will, all my rebellion, and my desire to stay away from people vanished. That night, after Eric said, "Don't ever stop praying," I surrendered to the Lord and told Him I was willing to do whatever He wanted me to do and go wherever He wanted me to go—on His terms.

Oh, what a relief to be free of rebellion, to let God be God. It was like the dawning of a bright new day in my life. It was the day for which God had patiently waited—the day my heart was made right.

Sometime later, we received a good report from Eric's mother. Doctors had examined Eric and found nothing wrong with his heart. He never had the open-heart surgery. God had healed him.

The Gift of Compassion

A great change came over me after I surrendered to the will of God. I felt so much better and happier. Bill felt a lot better too; he no longer had to endure my rebellion as he had all of those months.

We had become fast friends with some of the people in the Methodist church over in Bedford. They were charismatic and loved us and welcomed us to their fellowship. I wanted to attend that church. God had other ideas. The Lord would show Bill when I reached my coping limit at my own church. That's when we would visit the church in Bedford. Thank God, He eventually revealed to Bill how long we should remain at our original church.

The day after Kathryn Kuhlman died we were attending a meeting at our church. After the service concluded, the minister motioned for me to come over to where he was standing.

"I'm sorry to hear about Kathryn Kuhlman's death," he said.

I told him that Chris had just cried his heart out when he heard about her death. I told my pastor how I had tried to comfort Chris by telling him, "She's in Heaven now, Chris. I can just imagine her going in and saying, 'Oh, this is exactly the way I thought it would be. But that should be moved over here and this should be moved over there.' I can picture her rearranging Heaven."

After hearing what I had told Chris, my pastor looked at me in silence for a minute, then said, "That's not what I see."

"Oh?" I asked. Suddenly it was apparent that our conversation had become quite serious.

"I see her standing with the Lord and saying, 'Lord, there's one you used me to heal. There's Delores. Is she doing everything you would have her do?'"

His words stunned me.

Then I said, "Well, Pastor, if I'm not, I'm sure I will."

He nodded and that was the last conversation we ever had.

During Kathryn's illness, God gave me a great love and compassion for her. The Lord revealed to me what she was going through. I knew it wasn't easy for her. She was perhaps one of the greatest women of our century, one of God's chosen vessels. Had it not been for her, I would have died a hopeless invalid, never knowing the healing power of the Holy Spirit.

The last time we attended our Presbyterian church, the Lord moved on my heart; it was such a wonderful experience. Suddenly, I saw those people in the church through the eyes of Jesus. For the first time, I loved them and had compassion on them. It had brought me such pain and sorrow that they had rejected me and that they had never spoken openly of my healing. Yet that no longer bothered me. My heart held only love and compassion for them.

When we left the church that day, the lump in my stomach was gone, never to return. God kept us in that church all that time for my inner healing. Had I not learned to love those people and have compassion on them, God never could have used me to serve Him.

The Whole Loaf

God used Bill during all that time when I refused to listen to His call. I praise the Lord that He never gave up on me, even in all my rebellion.

Of course, I still had visions of staying home, cooking and taking care of my family. During that entire time, something else kept flashing through my mind—visions of ministry. I initially shut the door, not wanting to accept it. Bill knew what was happening. Until I surrendered, God used him to keep me moving in the right direction. I still had some rough times, but things got much better.

For instance, one day as I was speaking to a group, I saw Jesus. We were sitting in a large circle. As I looked across the room, Jesus was standing there. I knew it was Jesus because I could see Him so clearly. He was holding a huge loaf of bread in His outstretched hands. He was looking right at me.

I said, "Lord, I don't know what You're saying."

Suddenly, He turned toward me. I saw a deep hurt in His eyes and knew what He was saying.

"I bring a whole loaf like this for each one of you and all you do is take a little nibble. I have the whole loaf for you. Why aren't you taking it?" the Lord was asking.

The vision of Jesus and His probing question greatly puzzled me.

Then the Word of God spoke to me from Philippians 4:19, *"But my God shall supply all your need according to His riches in glory by Christ Jesus"* (KJV).

A question came to me: "What do you think it is like in Heaven? The angels praise Him without ceasing." The joy of Heaven is ours right here, but we have to reach out and take it. We must reach out and take the whole loaf—not just a few crumbs.

After seeing Jesus standing there before me holding the loaf of bread, I knew I had to take it all in order to be all He wanted me to be. So I did.

As I followed the leading of the Lord into a full-time ministry of salvation and healing, there were still some doubts in my mind. But God was gracious and patient. He answered every question and overcame every doubt.

Bill and I formed the Fellowship Foundation, Inc. while in Arlington. The organization would serve as the physical arm of our spiritual ministry.

For some time Bill and I had felt the inner urging to move to Shreveport, Louisiana, where we were to make our home. God had established a strong group of supporters there who pledged to assist us in our ministry.

Leaving Arlington was no easy decision. Our son Doug, his wife Ann, and our grandchildren lived nearby. Our move would take us farther away from them. Chris, 17 at the time, had lived in Arlington since the age of one. He would have to leave his roots, the only city and home he had ever known. Bill would have to resign his good job and take another job at half the pay. But God simply said, "This is the job I've ordained."

Also, there was the question of age. We felt we were too old to begin a full-time ministry. But we decided that if we were to receive the full loaf of bread Jesus had held out to us in the vision, we would have to do everything He wanted—not what we wanted. We were convinced it was His will for us to move. We stepped out in faith, determining to live one day at a time. We knew that God would take care of all our needs.

In 1976, God sends out Bill and Delores Winder for a healing ministry to His people.

God revealed to us that He was never going to leave us, and we would never be in need. If we walk with Him today, we are assured that He will take care of all our tomorrows.

Has He not promised: *"Lo, I am with you always, even unto the end of the world"* (Matt. 28:20)?

We accepted God's loving invitation to move to Shreveport. The days and years of ministry were placed squarely in the Lord's hands, for it was His ministry and we were blessed to be a part of it.

Chapter 7

THE MINISTRY

For John baptized with water,
but in a few days you will be baptized
with the Holy Spirit
(Acts 1:5).

Although I didn't realize it at the time, when God healed me on that unforgettable night, He also baptized me in the Holy Spirit. Then He bestowed on me the gift of healing as explained by the apostle Paul in the 12th chapter of First Corinthians.

Through the months, the Lord taught Bill and me the meaning of the baptism. Until we receive that baptism and are filled, we cannot consistently manifest the fruit of the Spirit.

God wants to get inside us and thoroughly clean us out. Without the baptism of the Holy Spirit, it is difficult to have the full joy of the Lord. That is the reason so many Christians are sad as they sit in church worship services on Sunday, not even knowing why.

You always know when you are with Spirit-filled Christians because there is so much joy among them. There is a light in their eyes that never goes out. Why? Because they have the fullness of the Spirit within them.

I had to receive the baptism when I was healed because I didn't know how to love people. Oh, I could sort of love those in my family and maybe someone in trouble. But I couldn't go up to someone, put my arms around him, and say, "I love you." Love is the basic fruit of the Spirit. God could not use me fully until I showed the love of Jesus for other people.

People ask me today, "Why do I need the baptism in the Holy Spirit?"

My answer is, "Because Jesus commanded us to receive the baptism. That makes us whole. Without it we cannot be whole." The baptism brings boldness for witnessing into our lives; it also brings healing for us. When our spirits are healed, it often results in physical healing.

Sandy's Miracle

Bill and I were no strangers to the ministry, just new in physical healing. During those long months of preparation, God already had performed some miraculous healings. I remember the first time I ever had to deal with a terminal patient.

Janice, a minister's wife, asked me if I would go with her to Houston, Texas, to pray for her friend Sandy, who was 26 years old and dying of cancer. Surgeons in West Texas, where Sandy lived, had removed one breast and performed a colostomy, allowing her bowels to move through a tube into a plastic bag attached to her side. From samples taken from her glands, the surgeons learned that she was eaten up with cancer, so they sent her over to M.D. Anderson Hospital to see if there was anything that could be done for her. It was there that radiologists discovered hot spots on her liver. The cancer had spread throughout her body.

Janice and I decided to drive to Houston, rent a room, and go to the hospital the next morning to pray for Sandy. However, when we arrived in Houston it was apparent that satan was trying to keep us from praying for her. There were so many conventions in the city that all of the hotels and motels were full. Since Janice was pregnant, due to have her baby at any time, we had to have a place to stay.

We thought perhaps we should return home, but suddenly—in my spirit—I knew we dare not go home. Satan was throwing obstacles in our way and didn't want us to pray for Sandy.

Janice had an aunt and uncle who lived in Houston; we thought we might stay with them. We called four times, but there was no answer. By 10:30 P.M., we were getting a little desperate.

Finally, I said to Janice, "We're staying in Houston if we have to sleep in the car. Even if you have the baby in the car, God will take care of us."

Janice agreed with that positive confession. The next time we called her aunt and uncle, they were at home and invited us to spend the night. The next morning, we went to M.D. Anderson Hospital to see Sandy.

When we arrived at her room, a nurse told us she had already been taken downstairs for tests and probably would be gone most of the day. We went into the room where her mother was waiting while the tests were being performed.

When we greeted her, she said, "They've just taken Sandy downstairs. You've missed her. She probably won't be back until late this afternoon."

"No, that's not right," I said. "We're going to pray."

We prayed and asked God to perform a miracle and bring Sandy back to the room. Then we waited. In just a few minutes, the elevator door opened and two orderlies wheeled Sandy back into her room.

She told us that, for some unknown reason, she had asked her doctors if she could return to her room for one hour, even though she did not know we were coming to visit her.

I took one look at her weakened condition and said, "God, I'm not talking to this girl about healing unless You show me in a definite way that I'm supposed to. She's just too near death."

Janice had brought three books to give to Sandy. Among them was *The Miracles*, written by Dr. Richard Casdorph, which included a chapter on my miraculous healing. She laid the books on a table beside Sandy's bed; *The Miracles* was between the other books. (See the Appendix for the complete chapter about my case.)

Sandy reached over, picked up the books, and started thumbing through them. She saw *The Miracles* and opened it.

"*The Miracles*. What's this about?" she asked.

"Sandy, it's about people who were healed," Janice replied.

"Oh," Sandy said and laid the book down.

I said to the Lord, "I'm sorry. That's not good enough for me. Not with this woman who's dying of cancer. You're going to have to show me something more definite than that."

A few minutes later Sandy again picked up *The Miracles,* opened it, and said, "Delores Winder—that's you. Were you healed?"

"Yes," I replied.

Then I said, "OK, Lord, I'll talk to her about healing."

So I told Sandy what God had done for me.

"You mean you were dying and you were healed?" she asked.

"Yes," I answered.

"That's really something," she said.

"Do you believe it?" I asked her.

"Yes, I do," she answered.

We prayed for her healing. By the time we finished the prayer, the orderlies had returned with a stretcher to take her back downstairs to continue the tests. As they were leaving the room, her husband arrived.

She talked to him for a minute or so and then looked back toward Janice and me and said, "Don't leave."

Both Janice and I noticed her face looked completely different.

"There's something different about her," Janice said.

"Yes, there is," I added.

The orderlies wheeled her downstairs, but kept her only a short time. Then they returned her to the room and put her back to bed.

As soon as the orderlies were gone, Sandy got out of bed and said, "I'm going to take a shower. I feel filthy and my hair is filthy."

A nurse who was walking by the door looked in and saw Sandy getting out of bed. She rushed into the room and said, "You can't do that!"

"Oh, yes I can," Sandy answered as she went into the bathroom. She turned on the shower and began singing as she washed her hair.

The nurse returned with two orderlies to help get Sandy back into bed. When they heard her singing in the shower they turned around and left.

She came out of the shower with a towel wrapped around her head and said, "I feel great!" Then she sat down on her bed.

Later that afternoon, the doctors sent for Sandy. They wanted to give her a report on the tests they had run after we had prayed for her that morning.

Before she left the room she said to me, "Don't leave—I need to have you here until we hear what the doctors have to say."

Again, they wheeled her downstairs where Sandy met with all 12 doctors who were working on her case.

The doctors were amazed and gave her the miraculous results. One doctor came out of the counseling room and said, "Did you hear that they couldn't find anything?"

"No," I answered, smiling.

"They found the cancer before, but they couldn't find it this time," the doctor added.

Sandy looked like a new woman when they brought her back to her room. It was a time of great rejoicing in the Lord! But one of the doctors said that she should go ahead and have chemotherapy. "Ask God to shut the door if He doesn't want you to have it," I told her.

That day she told the doctors she wanted to go to the apartment where her mother and husband were living while in Houston. The doctor consented but asked her to return in a few days for the chemotherapy. When she went back to the hospital on Thursday for the chemotherapy the Lord had closed the door through her own doctor. "Sandy, I think we'll wait until next Tuesday to start the treatment," he said.

Sandy continued to pray about whether she should have the chemotherapy treatments. When she went back to see the doctor on Tuesday, he took one look at her and said, "I don't want to do anything today. Why don't we send you home for three weeks? Then we will see how you are doing."

Several weeks later, Sandy came to my home and rang the doorbell. When I opened the door I didn't even recognize her.

"You don't know who I am, do you?" she said.

"No, I don't," was my reply.

"I'm Sandy," she said, smiling.

What a blessed thing it was to realize the goodness of God in healing her! It sent sensations of joy all through my body. Praise welled up in my heart.

The question is often asked of me, "Why are people so fearful of cancer?" I believe it is a serious tool of the devil, and he has caused people to be super fearful of it. Doctors build on that fear by saying, "Oh, it's cancer. There's nothing we can do." God has revealed to me that as far as His healing power is concerned, cancer is nothing more than a common cold. However, most people react to the disease with great fear. That fear is a great hindrance to their healing.

Healing, Miracles, and Salvation

During those early days, the Lord kept speaking to me, saying, "Keep the balance and educate My people."

That is everything! To have a good balance is the first priority in preaching the Gospel. Unfortunately, among Spirit-baptized believers today, there is not a strong enough emphasis on winning people to the

Lord. Many people want to see miracles; they get all excited, but soon forget that Jesus' first priority is to bring people into the Kingdom—not miracles, not healing, not deliverance, but *salvation.*

During all of our healing services, Bill and I emphasize that first priority—people must be saved. What good will healing do for people if they die and go to hell?

It amazes me how many church members are not saved. We meet them and deal with them all the time. We should never take a person's salvation for granted just because that person's name is on the church rolls.

Churches have become so socially oriented that many people who have joined are totally oblivious of the need to commit their lives to Jesus Christ. Remember that the word *salvation* relates to the whole person—body, soul, and spirit. It means salvation from sin and death, but it also includes healing and deliverance. Jesus came to minister to the whole person; we must follow His example.

As the word of my testimony spread, God opened doors for me to receive invitations from all over the country to minister His healing power.

During a women's meeting in Sarasota, Florida, some friends brought a woman to the service. She was so severely crippled that she had to be carried into the meeting place.

When I saw her friends carrying her in, I became a little irritated. Sometimes, well-meaning people will drag sick people into meetings when they really would rather not be there. But did God ever teach me something that day!

This woman was in such sad condition that anyone might've said the Lord couldn't heal her. She was debilitated. The people sitting beside her had to hold her up in her chair to keep her from falling to the floor.

I asked the Lord to let me forget she was there because my attention was all wrapped up in her sad condition rather than in ministering the Word to all the people.

After the teaching was completed, I called for those who wanted prayer to come to the altar.

Sure enough, here came those ladies carrying the helpless woman to the altar. I laid hands on her. She was slain in the Spirit. I continued ministering to the other ladies.

Four months later, I began getting reports about a woman who had been healed in the Sarasota meeting. Of course I didn't remember her name. Two years later, I met the woman at a Bible conference in Florida. She came running and jumping up to me and asked, "Delores, do you know who I am?"

"No, I don't think so," I replied.

"I'm Mary!" she exclaimed.

"That's good," I said. "It's nice to know you."

Then she said, "No, you don't understand. I'm the one who was healed in Sarasota!"

We rejoiced in the Lord together!

One night while ministering the Word at a Full Gospel Businessmen's meeting in Hope, Arkansas, we saw cataracts melt away from a woman's eyes. I have to confess that, when I first saw her eyes clouded with cataracts, I really didn't have the faith to believe she would be healed.

When she came to the altar for prayer, I laid hands on her and offered a simple supplication to the Lord for the cataracts to be taken away. Then I moved among the others standing at the altar and prayed for them, one by one.

A few minutes later someone took me by the arm, pointed toward the lady who had the cataracts, and said, "Come look at her eyes."

I looked and saw color in her eyes. Before, we had only seen a cloudy film. Her eyes continued to heal during the evening. When she went to church the next morning her eyes were completely clear. Praise be to God!

The wonderful people of the Lady of Fatima Catholic Church of Monroe, Louisiana, often invite Bill and me to minister there. God has poured out His Spirit on those people, and there have been a number of miracles of healing.

A woman with a large growth on her neck came for prayer during one of the meetings at Lady of Fatima. As I looked at the growth I could see that it was about the size of a large hen egg.

We laid hands on the woman. As we prayed for her the growth began to decrease in size, little by little, until it was completely gone. There was great rejoicing among those Charismatic Catholics as they witnessed the manifestation of the healing power of God!

Embracing the Holy Spirit's Ways

God had a lot of teaching to do in my life. At times, I was a slow learner. For instance, it took some doing for me to accept people being slain in the Spirit.

Sometime after my healing—when I was slain in the Spirit twice— I began to feel strange sensations in my hands, like electric currents going through them. It frightened me, for I sensed it was the power of

God flowing through me. For days, I kept my hands in my pockets, not wanting to touch anyone, fearing something strange might happen.

One day while teaching a Bible lesson to a group of women in Arlington, I took an elderly woman by the hand and she fell out in the Spirit. As I reached out to help her, I touched another woman and she fell out. Then I brushed against two other ladies and they both went down under the power of the Spirit.

Frightened, I started to run out of the meeting place, bumped into a woman in a wheelchair, and she fell out under the Spirit. Another woman backed into me and she went down.

I grabbed my keys and pocketbook and ran to my car. I went immediately to a Spirit-filled pastor whom I loved and trusted, to ask him what had happened.

"What were you doing when it happened?" the pastor asked me.

"Trying to get away," I replied.

Very carefully, he explained the purpose of God in taking people out under the power of the Spirit. He said God does it when He wants to minister to a person's spirit, to provide spiritual help for them. The pastor took me through various Scriptures that shed light on the question.

He explained that during a post-resurrection appearance of Jesus, the phenomenon occurred when the keepers of the sepulcher saw the angel, his raiment white as snow. The Word says: *"And for fear of him the keepers did shake, and became as dead men"* (Matt. 28:4).

Also, the pastor explained John 18:3-6 to me. The passage begins with Judas bringing the officers and chief priests to the Garden of Gethsemane to arrest Jesus. The men were carrying lanterns and torches and weapons.

When Jesus asked them, *"Whom seek ye?"* they answered, *"Jesus of Nazareth"* (John 18:4-5 KJV).

The Word says: *"As soon then as He had said unto them, I am He, they went backward, and fell to the ground"* (John 18:6 KJV).

The pastor explained that on another occasion a father brought to Jesus his son who had a dumb spirit. When Jesus ministered deliverance to the boy, Mark 9:26 says: *"And the spirit cried, and rent him sore, and came out of him: and he was as one dead; insomuch that many said, He is dead"* (KJV).

The pastor told me about how, when the silver-haired apostle John saw the vision on the Isle of Patmos, he *"...fell at His feet as dead..."* as noted in Revelation 1:17 (KJV).

Also, the pastor said that in Daniel 8:18 when the young prophet saw a vision, he recorded these words: *"Now as he was speaking with me, I was in a deep sleep on my face toward the ground: but he touched me and set me upright"* (KJV).

Praise God for that Spirit-filled pastor! He helped me so much that day! All my fears of this spiritual phenomenon vanished and never returned.

He suggested that I try to find out what God had done for those women who were slain in the Spirit in the meeting that day. Later, I asked each one of them what had happened while they were out under the power of the Spirit. One lady told me she had not wept for 12 years, yet when she came out from under the power, she wept freely.

Another lady said she had never before felt the love of God. When slain in the Spirit that day, she said she felt cushioned in the arms of Jesus and heard Him telling her He loved her. One of the other ladies received a healing and another received the baptism in the Holy Spirit while out under the power of God. After speaking with those dear women, I better understood what God had done.

At times there still were doubts in my mind about it, until one day I heard the voice of God saying to me, "You take care of your business, and I'll take care of this." Now I leave it completely in His hands.

Chapter 8

THE GREAT PHYSICIAN

Jesus went through all the towns and villages…
preaching the good news of the kingdom
and healing every disease and sickness
(Matthew 9:35).

One night while I was ministering in a Presbyterian church in Shreveport, an unusual prayer request was made by a Spirit-filled minister. He said one of his friends, an attorney, had gone to St. Luke's Hospital in Houston for cardiovascular surgery. The minister volunteered to stand in proxy for his friend as I prayed for him.

Everyone in the service felt the power of the presence of God as we laid hands on the Spirit-filled minister. That night, the Lord gave us the assurance that the attorney was healed.

The attorney later related the following story to us: Some weeks before we had prayed for him, he had sensed numbness in his right thigh. He immediately went to see an orthopedic surgeon who was unable to find a pulse in his thigh, groin, and ankle. The doctor concluded that the large blood supply to the right leg had become blocked and suggested that the attorney be hospitalized immediately.

While he was in the hospital, the doctor called in several specialists, including a reputable cardiovascular surgeon, to confirm his findings. Not one of the specialists could find a pulse. The consensus among the four physicians was that the attorney must have surgery.

Arrangements were made with Dr. Denton Cooley, the famed Houston heart surgeon, to perform the operation at St. Luke's. Meanwhile, hundreds of people were called into prayer for the attorney, including those who laid hands on the man in proxy in our service at the Presbyterian church.

The attorney checked into St. Luke's and underwent extensive testing. A few days later, just before the surgery, a young resident entered the attorney's room. The resident asked the attorney, "Mind if I see if I can find a pulse in your leg?"

"Of course, go ahead," the attorney replied.

After briefly examining the leg, the young resident said, "I'm not so sure about your vascular problem, but you see that's not my job."

Then Dr. Cooley, accompanied by six other doctors, visited the attorney for a pre-operation examination. After checking the attorney very carefully, Dr. Cooley told him he did not need surgery, but he suggested that a neurologist conduct another examination just for confirmation.

The neurologist gave the attorney a thorough examination and agreed with Dr. Cooley that no surgery was necessary. The attorney praised the Lord, for he knew that God had healed him! He knew the Great Physician had touched him.

When he returned home, he went back to his own doctor and told him the story of what had happened. His doctor checked him and found a strong pulse in his leg.

"How could I have missed the pulse?" he asked the attorney. "I would take an oath that it wasn't there before."

"You didn't miss it," the attorney replied. "I've had hundreds, maybe thousands of people praying for me. God made this old body and He knows how to repair it."

Many Believers…Many Ministers

While ministering one evening in that same Presbyterian church in Shreveport, I noticed a Catholic nun in the audience. The church was filled with people who were searching for healing of their afflictions, but I kept noticing the Catholic sister, who was probably in her early 60s. That night, I felt impressed of the Lord to invite her to the platform to minister with me. She agreed.

There was a woman with a large growth on her face standing at the altar for prayer. I asked the sister, "Do you want to minister healing? Would you pray with this woman?"

"I don't know how; I've never done that before," the sister whispered to me.

"Would you like to pray for her?" I asked again.

"Yes, I'll try," she replied.

"No, you'll do, not *try*. You'll do your part, and God will do the rest," I explained.

"All right," she said.

She laid her hand on the growth on the woman's cheek and prayed. When she took her hand away the growth was gone. The very first time the Catholic sister prayed for someone to be healed, God performed a great miracle through her!

This is such a great day for the Church because God is pouring out His Spirit on all flesh!

The day is before us when we will see more and more churches carrying out the full ministry of Jesus. When this takes place, there will no longer be any need for a ministry such as mine. The healing ministry will have returned to the Church where it belongs. Our Lord's perfect will is for the pastors to stand strong in the pulpits throughout this nation to proclaim the full Gospel.

You recall that I was in church all my life prior to my many years of illness. During those years, not one minister ever prayed that I would be healed. They prayed only that I would be able to endure the suffering and pain. And did I ever endure it!

But that is not the prayer Jesus taught us. He said He would heal His people and deliver us. When we know what God has available for us, then we can come to Him and ask for it. But we don't keep on asking. We start appropriating what He has promised. We say, "Lord, although I still have pain in my body, I believe that You are healing me because Your Word says You will."

Then our physical body begins to change as the mind, body, and spirit come into one accord with God's Word. The best way for us to be healed is to be in accord with His Word, for it is basically through His Word that we hear from Him.

All Spirit-baptized believers can hear God's call to minister. The gifts of the Spirit can operate in a downtown office building just as in a healing and miracle service. Many people have never caught on to that truth. The gifts should be in operation wherever we are and whatever we are doing in our daily lives.

Bill and I are just two people, but the Lord has graciously allowed our ministry to touch thousands. I see the thousands, yea millions, of Spirit-baptized believers who work in downtown office buildings, factories, hospitals, government offices. If they would catch the vision of ministry where they work, it would be a bright new day for the Kingdom of God.

Homemakers can also minister. Be sure to teach your children about Jesus and to minister to them. They receive so quickly. Once, when Bill and I were guests in the home of some friends, their little girl jumped up in my lap and said, "Delores, my nose is stopped up and I can't breathe very good and can't sleep. Would you pray for me?"

Her parents were talking long distance on the telephone, so I prayed, "Jesus, you know that Kimmy has to get some sleep. I'm just going to ask You to open up her nose and clear her sinuses so that she can sleep. Thank You." Kimmy said, "Whew. Thank you," and went to bed and to a deep sleep.

Children readily receive, but mothers and fathers often don't bother to pray for them when they are sick. Yet some of those same mothers and fathers may be considered very spiritual people. Often, they are out ministering to others while neglecting the ministry to their own children in the home. It only takes a minute to allow the love of Jesus and His healing power to touch a child.

People who have witnessed great miracles and have seen the healing power of God should stay excited about what God can do for the healing of their children. Sometimes all we have is the name of Jesus. I've known mothers who would sit by the bed of a sick child and just repeat the name of Jesus. You could see that child being healed.

Not long before this writing, Bill and I ministered in Massachusetts, New Hampshire, and Ohio. God performed many wonderful miracles during those meetings. In Ohio, a man with a tumor on his spine came for ministry. The x-ray clearly revealed the tumor; his surgeons had told him it had to be removed. We prayed a simple prayer for his healing and God touched him.

When he went to the hospital for surgery, the surgeon decided to x-ray his spine again before the operation. The x-rays startled the surgeon, for the tumor was gone. The man rejoiced in the healing power of our wonderful Lord.

Also in Ohio, a woman who had been confined to a wheelchair for three years came to the services. During the meeting, the Lord spoke to me and said someone in the audience could rise up and walk. He didn't tell me who it was, but He did reveal it to Bill. Bill went to the woman in the wheelchair and said, "You can get up now." She got up and walked and praised the Lord!

God also healed a Florida woman of multiple sclerosis. When she came into our meeting, she was in such bad condition that the toes on one of her feet were doubled under. We prayed for her. Then I said, "Come on, let's walk."

She stood up, but then sat back down saying, "My toes are cramping." We took off her shoes and watched as her toes began to unfold. They continued straightening out until she was totally healed. Before her healing, we had sensed blackness around her. Now she is a radiant Christian through whom the love of the Lord shines brightly.

Oh, the wonders of our Lord! How He wants to heal His people. He already has provided everything needed for that healing. All we must do is receive it. Every day, He proves that He is the Great Physician.

Chapter 9

Inner Healing

He heals the brokenhearted
and binds up their wounds
(Psalm 147:3).

The late State Senator Talbot Fields of Arkansas was in a lot of trouble with the law. He was on trial in his home state and facing a long prison sentence. A friend told him about our ministry and one day, during his trial, he called me from Arkansas.

After introducing himself and telling me a little about his problems, he said, "I want you to pray for me. I'm in trouble and it looks like I'm going to jail. Everything is lost."

As we began to pray, suddenly I saw the Lord breaking him free. The Lord showed the senator that he would not go to prison. We had a real hallelujah time right there on the telephone.

When the judge later dismissed the charges against him, Senator Fields raised his hands in the courtroom and praised God, confessing that it was by His power that he was a free man.

Sometime later, I received a letter from the senator's wife. She said that as the senator and I prayed on the telephone, he received an inner healing. This set him free from the chains that had bound his spirit. She did not elaborate, nor did I inquire as to the nature of the inner healing. That was between the senator and God.

Senator Fields has since passed away, but during his last years here on earth he proved he was a remarkable man. After he was healed inwardly, God provided a way out of his legal entanglements, apparently assured that the senator would straighten up his life and be a good risk. The judge thought so, too.

Senator Fields became the founder and president of the Full Gospel Businessmen's Chapter in Hope, Arkansas. He invited me to minister at one of the chapter's meetings. He praised the Lord during the waning days of his life and never failed to testify that it was God who set him free—inside and outside.

God's Word has a lot to say about inner healing. Jesus Himself said He came to earth to heal the brokenhearted—that's inner healing. The Book of Proverbs is full of good advice on how we can stay well inwardly, spiritually.

The Benefits of a Clean Heart

As you study the Proverbs, you begin to understand that our spirits cannot be full of such things as anger, hatred, resentment, and bitterness and remain full of the Holy Spirit. We often try to close the Lord out of our lives by allowing all kinds of inner afflictions to overtake us.

There are going to be brief times in our lives when we may feel anger, resentment, frustration, and unforgiveness. But these only linger if we fail to lay them at the foot of the cross. We are the ones who suffer if we allow such dangerous emotions to hang around.

During these years of ministry, I've met many, many people who carry unforgiveness in their hearts. It is the most devastating of all inner emotions. Anyone who cannot control that emotion must say: "Lord, I lay it down and I forgive that person through You. Even if I can't do it by myself right now, I'm going to forgive that person because You forgave them. Now I'm asking You to give me the kind of feelings I should have in my heart."

This is the cleaning out process. This is inner healing.

Medical science acknowledges that much physical sickness comes from spiritual sickness. For instance, when a person tells a lie, certain glandular secretions attack the stomach and can, over a period of time, make a person sick.

The Lord showed me one day that it is as though we have "valleys" inside us. When all our resentment, hatred, bitterness, and other harmful emotions settle into those valleys, we often think, "This will pass and I'll forget it."

That is a dangerous assumption. When we forget something, it only means that the issue has been exiled to the subconscious. Hidden away, a little scab forms over the memory and seals it; but it will continue festering there.

Jesus wants to peel the scab away, clean out the valley, and allow the Holy Spirit to fill it with good things. Essentially, psychiatry seeks to accomplish through physical means what God does through spiritual means.

There was a woman in her 70s who attended one of our meetings in Florida. Crippled with arthritis, she came to the altar for prayer during the invitation. I don't believe in blanket prayers such as, "God, heal them." When I face someone in need, I pray, "Lord, show me their need."

Often I don't even hear what a person is saying; their request may not represent their real need, but may be the result of the real need. In the case of the woman who came for healing of arthritis, the Lord spoke to me the word *unforgiveness.*

"Is there someone you need to forgive or to ask forgiveness of?" I asked her.

There was a sweet expression on her face as she said, "No." I wanted to believe her; she looked like such an honest, sincere person. But the Lord said, "No—unforgiveness."

So I asked her again, "Is there someone you need to forgive or ask forgiveness of?"

"No," she answered, a puzzled expression on her face.

"It just can't be," I thought, for she appears so confused at my questions.

As I began praying for her, the Lord spoke to me again: "I said *unforgiveness.* Don't pray a general prayer. I said *unforgiveness.*"

I stopped praying and said to her, "I'm sorry, but the Lord is showing me there is unforgiveness in your life."

Tears started rolling down her cheeks, and I felt as though I was badgering her. Yet, the Lord had spoken; I had to stand on what He said. Finally, I said, "Lord, You're going to have to show me what to do."

Then the Lord spoke the word *brother.*

So I asked her, "What about your brother?"

She looked as though to burn holes through me.

"You do have a brother?" I asked.

"Yes," she replied.

"Is there a problem between you?" I questioned.

"No," she replied.

"Has there been a problem between you?" I asked.

Then she said emphatically, "No! I *x'd* him out of my life a long time ago!"

I was shocked.

"What do you mean you *x'd* him out of your life?"

"I just *x'd* him out," she said.

"Because you had a problem?" I questioned.

"Yes, but it doesn't bother me," she replied.

"Look at your hands, your legs, your feet. Do you want to get rid of this arthritis?" I asked. "Then you are going to have to forgive your brother or ask his forgiveness," I told her.

She glared at me.

"Do you want to be free from your arthritis?" I asked.

"Yes," she said.

But for a minute she had some questions in her mind as to whether she wanted to pay such a price to be healed. She wasn't sure the price was worth it.

"Are you willing to forgive him? Will you ask him to forgive you?" I asked.

"Yes," she answered.

"How long have you had this arthritis?" I inquired.

"About 12 years," she said.

"When was it that you and your brother had your problem?" I asked.

"It's been about 12 years," she replied.

Then it hit her like a bomb! Suddenly she realized what she had just said.

"You are going to forgive him because the Lord spoke it," I said.

"Yes," she said.

Then I prayed with her and said, "Now you are going to have to either write or call your brother and talk to him about this. Tell him you have forgiven him and ask him to forgive you," I instructed.

"No, I don't have to do that," she informed me.

"Yes, you do," I emphasized.

"No, I won't need to call or write him—he only lives two doors away from me," she said.

Only two doors away, yet full of bitterness toward each other for 12 years! And the bitterness caused her to be crippled with arthritis.

Later, a friend who knew the situation between the woman and her brother explained the problem to me. Their fight with each other was over a mere $3,000 that each of them thought they should have received when their mother died.

This friend told me, "That woman is so rich she could buy or sell half of this city."

What a tragedy for a wealthy woman to suffer arthritis because she felt her brother had cheated her out of $3,000.

Let me say a word of caution about inner healing: after you receive it, satan will try to bring the problem back. Even though you are free of it, the evil one will whisper the thought of it in your ear. Then you must take authority and say, "No, satan. Praise God I'm free of it because of Jesus."

There are also times when God gives inner healing through weeping. Some people just cry it out. A friend of mine wept for six weeks after he was saved. It took that long for the Holy Spirit to clean out all the guilt that had built up in him through the years. At the end of six weeks of weeping, he was set free.

The beautiful thing is that God knows how uniquely He made each one of us and He deals with us in different ways. That is why I don't like blanket prayers. God does not deal with us that way. I want to hear God speaking to me as I minister. Only then will I know, through the person's uniqueness, how God wants to deal with them.

Inner Healing and Freedom

There was another woman who received a miraculous inner healing. Her problem was fear. It constantly ripped her apart and caused emotional and even mental problems. For years, she had lived in a state of depression. She had shock treatments—the works—but nothing helped.

When we prayed for her, the Lord set her free. Now she is such a joy to the Lord and to her friends. She is just bubbly all the time. She works in a large office building, and the Lord has given her a ministry of healing. A co-worker in her office will say to her, "I have a headache, will you go to the rest room and pray with me?"

The two will then take a trip to the rest room. There, the woman prays for the sick. Invariably, they are healed. She is so happy in that ministry.

Not once has she ever said, "Oh, I just think God is going to take me out of here and put me in a full-time ministry." She knows she is where God wants her to be. She is ministering to people and witnessing to the Lord right where she is. Even the men in her office come to her for prayer.

You know, I'll probably never work in a downtown office building. God needs ministers there eight hours a day, 40 hours a week. What a joy it would be for people to realize that the gifts of God are for all Christians, to be ministered everywhere.

A friend of mine told me a beautiful story of his wife's inner healing of bad memories. She carried bitterness in her heart toward a friend, and it bothered her so much that she could not sleep. One night, she prayed that the Lord would forgive her and help her to forget her bitterness toward her friend. The next morning, she awakened and remembered praying for the healing of the memory, but she could no longer remember the one against whom she had held the bitterness.

Unforgiveness is such a destructive emotion. When this sin grips you, it can cause your whole world to become topsy-turvy. Jesus, you recall, had quite a bit to say about the subject.

Let me share with you a little spiritual exercise I've learned about dealing with unforgiveness. Just pray, "Lord, I want to lay it down. I'm going to forgive that person through Jesus. If I can't do it by myself right now, I'll forgive because Jesus paid the price for it. I'll forgive through You. And I'm asking You to give me the kind of feelings I should have in my heart."

God promises us in His Word that after our sins are forgiven He remembers them no more. He completely forgets them. His attitude toward those sins is that they never existed.

There are times when we have trouble forgiving and forgetting our own sins. If God does not remember our sins, who is it that reminds us of them? The devil, of course. Often it requires inner healing to be able to forgive ourselves and forget past sins.

A friend of mine spent several years in prison, but now is saved and a powerful witness for Jesus. Some time ago an acquaintance asked him, "What were you in prison for?"

The former prisoner replied, "Listen, God has forgotten all about that, and I'm not going to give the devil a chance to bring it back up. It's covered in the blood of Jesus."

That's right! God forgave and forgot his sins. Why shouldn't he?

Inner healing deals with deep-seated emotions that go awry, often buried deep within us. Hurts, fears, resentment, anger, unforgiveness, doubt, bitterness, bad memories, phobias, and a lot of other problems need the touch of the hand of God.

When we carry these harmful emotions too long, we sometimes invite demons and unclean spirits into us. Demonic oppression can make a Christian as miserable as one who is possessed. And it is almost always the Christian who wants to be set free from demonic oppression, not the unbeliever. You recall that one time Jesus called an unclean spirit out of a man in the synagogue. Since the man was in the synagogue, he must have been worshiping God.

Inner healing takes place through a supernatural act of God. There is nothing hokey-pokey about it. What appears supernatural to us is natural with God; we must allow it to be the same with us as we walk in the Spirit.

There are some ministers who have hang-ups about women preachers, particularly Charismatic women preachers. This may require inner healing of attitudes toward women God has called into the ministry.

There was a young minister, the pastor of one of the largest churches in a metropolitan city, who came to our services. He held a doctor of theology degree and was just a typical, proud young man. He was handsome, brilliant, and pastor of a large church—the apex of success. Also, he was being groomed for a high position of leadership within his denomination.

The young minister knew the Word, at least the printed Word, and was a gifted, talented, anointed preacher. His preaching brought people to salvation in tears; yet, he preached only the Word and did not resort to emotional chicanery.

But this pastor had a problem: his little girl was sick with a dread disease. Suddenly, he faced a problem for which he had no answer. His inability to deal with the illness dealt a severe blow to his pride, haughtiness, and arrogance.

As his daughter's condition worsened, God began to give him a glimpse of something new in his experience. One day he opened the newspaper and saw my picture along with an advertisement stating I would be ministering in a Presbyterian church in his city.

He later told me that when he saw my picture the Lord spoke to him, but he didn't understand what it all meant. Every time he saw my picture in the paper he was pulled by some inner urging, but he only laughed at the idea.

One day he drove down to the grocery store to pick up a loaf of bread for his wife. On the way to the store he turned on the car radio and picked up my radio broadcast. He reached to turn off the program. Then he had a change of heart and said, "I'm going to listen to her to see if I understand anything she says." When he arrived at the store, he sat and waited in the car until the program was completed.

He returned home, not realizing what was happening to him. He had a strong feeling in his heart that he should call me. He called our office and said he wanted to see me, but I was out of town. It wasn't time for us to talk; he wasn't ready.

He said that during the seven months afterward it seemed that every time he turned on the radio he picked up our program. One day a layman in his church went to the pastor and told him he should take his daughter to one of our meetings. To the layman's great surprise, they came to our meeting the next night.

We received a call saying they would be there. I told them I would pray with his daughter before the service was to begin. One of the things the Lord has taught me is to be careful with people, particularly ministers, not to flaunt them or put them in precarious positions. Prior to the service I prayed for the little girl, so there was no spectacle made out of her well-known father being in our service.

They remained for the teaching. During the invitation, the young minister came to the altar and stood there in prayer. That night, the Lord broke a proud man. Then he and his wife brought their precious little girl to the altar. His beautiful wife was a timid person; I could only imagine what it cost her to come to the altar that night.

After the service he said, "I need to talk to you."

A few days later, we set up an appointment, and I shared with him the wonderful things God was doing. He openly received it all and said, "I know this is of the Lord."

God continued to break him. His little daughter became worse. Then he came to the point where he said to the Lord, "Anything and everything—I'm yours." A short time later, God blessed him with the baptism in the Holy Spirit, with the evidence of speaking in tongues.

He once told me, "Delores, I know that God had to break everything in me until I reached the point where I could look around my home and church and say, 'If this isn't where God wants me, I don't want to be here.' If He wants me living above a store with orange crates for furniture or preaching on the street corners of this world, I'm willing."

The young minister did a 180-degree turn. He is totally different now. All the material things, all the prominence of being the pastor of a large, influential church is gone. He now is one of the most powerful preachers I've ever heard.

The Lord spoke to him and said that his daughter would be healed, saying, "Her healing is set." He and his wife are standing on that promise.

Meanwhile, in a camp meeting in another state, God spoke to one of his friends saying that, if he would stand and ask the 1,000 people at the camp meeting to pray for the little girl, she would be healed.

That was the confirmation. Isn't it good of Jesus to do that for us? Remember, some people are not healed immediately. I don't know why. Sometimes it's just not God's time. We are never going to see a healing before God's timing is right—it could have disastrous consequences.

Inner healing sets us free and, as God's Word promises, when the Lord sets you free you are free indeed (see John 8:36).

Chapter 10

DELIVERANCE

These signs will accompany those who believe:
In My name they will drive out demons...
(Mark 16:17).

Some people need deliverance, particularly if there is sin or addiction in their lives, or if they have dabbled in the occult.

While there are many causes of emotional and mental illness, there are times when evil spirits cause these illnesses that disrupt a person's life.

One of the most sinister spirits we encounter is that of voodoo, a strong spirit that often comes into people through family ties.

A woman with a contorted body came into one of our meetings in Texas. She was physically misshapen. We laid hands on the deformed, twisted woman and called out the spirit of voodoo. The evil spirit fled and the woman was set free.

Usually the spirit of voodoo will try to choke a victim; the person's neck will swell up, cutting off the breath. Those ministering to such a person often become fearful when they see the person beginning to choke. It is necessary to take authority over the evil spirit, call it out and send it away.

On another occasion, a refined, well-educated woman came to a meeting where we were ministering. As we looked at the woman, we had no idea what we would be dealing with later. After the meeting, she came up to me and said she needed help. The Lord quickened me. I knew she needed deliverance, so we set a time when I would meet with her. The Lord also impressed me that a man should accompany me to her home for the ministry of deliverance. A local pastor and I went to her beautiful home.

The Lord then quickened me to call out the fear of her father. "Are you afraid of your father?" I asked her.

"No, I'm not afraid of him," she replied.

I looked at her for a moment and said, "I'm sorry. I've got to call it out."

As we began to pray and call out the spirit of fear of her father, her body started shaking just like a motor was running inside her. She grabbed the sides of the chair in which she was sitting. Her body started rising up until she was about 12 inches above the chair. Then she started bellowing like a wounded bull. The bellowing was so loud it would hit the fireplace and bounce back throughout the room.

My hair stood on edge and I shivered. Then the pastor and I called out the spirit of fear and control by her father, as well as the spirit of voodoo and all connected spirits. That was when I learned that anyone ministering deliverance must know and believe in the power of God. The evil spirits, bound in the name of Jesus, came out of her and left the house.

She later told me an incredible story of why she was afraid of her father. He had practiced voodoo for many years. On two occasions, he had cast spells on people, killing them when they tried to stand in the way of his promotions in his profession.

After her deliverance, she fully understood why the spirits had come into her. She had witnessed what her father could do to others through voodoo and was afraid that if she ever stepped out of line, her father would kill her, too. Once delivered from the evil spirits, the woman began to grow in the Lord. Today, she leads a Bible study group.

Common Demonic "Entryways"

Drugs are always demonic. A young boy came into one of our meetings so fogged he could hardly speak. He just kept staring at us, crazed-looking. When I spoke to him, it took a long time and a great struggle just for him to answer. When I touched the boy, he fell under the power of God and was delivered instantly from drug addiction.

Although people don't realize it, they often open themselves up to spirits of witchcraft by fooling around with tarot cards or Ouija boards—even by reading horoscopes in the newspapers. (Horoscopes are pure astrology.) Watching movies and television shows, as well as reading books about witchcraft and the occult are other openings for demons.

Oppression of a Christian or possession of a non-Christian takes place easily, so quietly that the person doesn't even notice it is happening. This is what people who have been delivered of demons and addictions tell me.

Once while ministering deliverance to a young woman, I heard her speaking with a man's voice. I called out the spirit of psychic power.

Then a deep, guttural voice said to me, "You don't want me to come out of her. If I come out of her, I'll come into you. I know you well."

As the demon spoke to me I backed away, frightened. Yet I knew the demon had to be cast out. Then the Lord said to me, "You'll do it or you'll always be afraid."

So I spoke to the demon and said, "No, I'm not afraid of you. You'll not come into me. You've never been in me." Then I called the demon out in the name of Jesus. The demon came out with a wailing moan.

"Get out of this place!" I ordered. The demon left.

There was a child who walked in darkness who was brought to me for deliverance. I was told that his mother was a prostitute. God revealed to me that the child needed deliverance and a healing of memories, even from the womb. He was born into a kingdom of darkness—his mother and grandfather both were involved in witchcraft.

I prayed with the boy for the healing of memories and commanded the unclean spirit, which had nearly destroyed him, to depart in the name of Jesus. Later we received a report on his progress. Now the little boy can walk and talk. He can even say, "I love Jesus."

Jesus has given believers authority over demons and unclean spirits. We exercised that authority on behalf of the little boy.

The devil is vicious—so vicious that he even attacks little children. Parents need to take authority over their little ones to protect them from such attacks.

One of our close friends, who often visits in our home, told us an incredible story of how the devil tried to attack his three-year-old daughter. Our friend is a former newspaper editor and often arrived home late in the evenings.

His wife began telling him of strange things that had been happening in the house: hanging lights would begin to sway back and forth; chairs would turn around right in front of her. One night she heard their daughter scream and rushed into her bedroom. The child was in a panic. She looked up at her mother with pleading eyes and said, "Mommy, he said he was going to kill me!"

"Who said that, sweetheart?" the mother asked.

"He did," the little girl answered, pointing toward the ceiling of the room.

That evening when the father returned home from the newspaper, he and his wife prayed for the child's deliverance from the tormentor and in the name of Jesus cast him out of her room. They also anointed the windows and doors of the room with oil, symbolic of the consecrating and protective power of the Holy Spirit over the child.

Later that evening, the three-year-old child called the mother into the room and said, "It's all right now—Jesus took care of him."

Thank God for parents who know how to provide spiritual protection for their children and to consecrate and take authority over the homes God has given them.

Let me also mention that a Christian can minister deliverance to himself. It is not the easiest way, but it can be done.

I never take deliverance lightly. Before getting into it, I always want to know three things:

First, is the need for deliverance or for discipline? Often people come to us and ask that we pray for them to be delivered from the spirit of nicotine. There is an evil spirit of nicotine, but I want to make sure the evil spirit is the root of the problem.

Second, has the person done everything in his power to break the habit?

Third, has the person prayed to Jesus and asked for the discipline necessary to break the bad habit?

One of the biggest problems among Charismatic Christians is that they don't seem to want to be disciplined. They want everything to be instant: healing, inner healing, or deliverance. Yet Jesus, who is our model, was the most disciplined man who ever walked the face of this earth.

There are a lot of Christians who won't discipline themselves; therefore they are not set free from certain bad habits. They attribute their habits to demons or unclean spirits when, in fact, the source is their undisciplined flesh.

When a person honestly answers these questions, saying he or she has done everything possible to be set free, then I know a demon is at work in that person's life and deliverance is necessary. I then bind the demon and call it out in the name of Jesus.

While some people want to be set free the easy way or want a "quickie" ministry of deliverance, there are people who no longer have any control over certain areas of their lives, such as lust.

There was a husband, a very gentle man, who often went into uncontrollable rages. This was totally against his character and his personality. Rage would overtake him, causing him to throw things around the house, even slap his loving wife.

He came to me and admitted his was not normal behavior. He said he could always tell when the rage was grabbing him. He would fight for days to keep it under control, then suddenly it would control him.

The demon in the man was bound, called out in the name of Jesus, and the gentle man was set free.

When something controls you and makes you do things that go against your personality and your beliefs, then you have a demon lodged in there, and it must be cast out in order for you to be free.

For too many years, Christians did not even realize that demons existed, and therefore did not guard against them. They are such evil creatures and they are always looking for a body to enter.

Many people have allowed and even unwittingly invited demons into their lives. But now we understand more about demons and must get rid of any that are in us. Thank God we have the authority in the name of Jesus and the power of the Holy Spirit to cast them out. Always remember, demons cannot stand for long when bound and called out in the precious name of Jesus. That is our inheritance as Christians!

Chapter 11

HEALING AND RECONCILIATION

He said to them, "Go into all the world
and preach the good news to all creation....
And these signs will accompany those who believe:
In My name they will drive out demons...
they will place their hands on sick people,
and they will get well"
(Mark 16:15; 17-18).

Healing is a gift of God ordained for His children. All throughout the Scriptures our Lord speaks healing to His people. He promises it to them. The provision God made for His people was intended primarily for their health, rather than their healing. God wants us to live and walk in divine health.

Because of the fall of man—the original sin—sickness came into the world. It has touched every person who ever lived, except Jesus. We who are God's people must learn how to combat that sickness or it will surely destroy us. Or, if we become ill, we must learn how to depend on the Lord for our healing. The first step toward healing is reconciliation—first to God, then to others.

Perhaps the apostle Paul penned the most definitive statement on the meaning of reconciliation. He wrote *"that God was reconciling the world to Himself in Christ, not counting men's sins against them. And He has committed to us the message of reconciliation"* (2 Cor. 5:19).

Let me remind you that when humanity fell from grace as a result of the original sin, our souls were infected with sin. This separated us from God spiritually. Because our bodies also fell out of grace, we have sickness. So Jesus is the instrument whereby our souls can be saved—and also whereby our bodies can be healed.

Here is how it works:

The Word tells us: *"Man that is born of a woman is of few days, and full of trouble"* (Job 14:1 KJV). That single verse sums up the history of humankind. People always seem to be in some degree of trouble, either with God or with other people.

Of course, there are always going to be differences among people because God made each of us unique; but those differences don't mean that war is the assumed outcome. They mean we must love each other a little more.

Before we can do that, we must be reconciled with God. In other words, we must be in right relationship with Him. Through Jesus we are forgiven for our sins and then reconciled to God. When we are reconciled, all the blessings for which Jesus paid the price are poured out to us.

But that's not all. Jesus established a line of communication between God and man. One of the basic blessings of that new relationship is prayer. No matter what I am doing, I'm always praying. While driving the car, I'm praying. While taking a load of laundry to the washing machine, I'm praying.

Most of us have barely touched the tip of these blessings because we haven't opened ourselves up to the Lord and to the full meaning of reconciliation. As we open up to Jesus, the Holy Spirit shows us the blessings available to us. That is when healing floods through us.

Reconciliation and the Roots of Illness

Now let's look at illnesses—spiritual, emotional, mental, and physical. Illness can come upon us when we are separated from God and chained by sin. The way we can get rid of that sickness is to get right with God, to be cleansed of personal sin in our lives through repentance.

There are many kinds of illness, but the most sinister ones come about when the emotions go awry. When dealing with emotional illness, we usually have to go back through the years with the individual to find the first occurrence or root of the illness.

Science has revealed that from the time of conception a child has awareness, even while in the womb. So, while praying with a person with emotional needs, you may have to pray for the healing of those very earliest memories.

I have learned there is very little I can do to assist in the healing process, so I simply walk the person through that process with Jesus. As a person allows Jesus to begin the healing, the Holy Spirit brings forth memories that have festered in the person's subconscious, memories of which the person may not be consciously aware. This is called *healing of memories.*

There are times when God gives me a picture as I minister healing of memories. One day as I ministered to a woman experiencing deep emotional distress, she said she had no idea why she was suffering emotionally. She told me her father was an alcoholic.

Suddenly, in the Spirit, I saw the picture of a child. I knew she was four years old and I saw her sitting in the middle of a bed, screaming. She had her arms over her face as though trying to hide. As I described the details of the scene to the woman, suddenly she said, "Stop!"

"What happened in that room?" I asked her.

Then she remembered. Her father was beating her mother in front of her. She was holding her arms over her eyes to keep from watching the cruel incident. The memory was buried so deep in the woman's subconscious that it created emotional distress and depression. When we finally brought it forth, she saw that Jesus was with her, holding her in His arms and protecting her. She also began to realize that He could heal her of the emotional suffering. And He did, praise God!

She later told me she always harbored bad feelings toward her father, but had never really understood why. She confessed that she had followed in her father's footsteps and become a heavy drinker herself.

After the Lord set her free, she knew the next step was to go to her father to help set him free. When she shared with him what the Lord had done in her life, it had an amazing impact. He received her testimony, and it led to his conversion and rapid spiritual growth.

She was set free from the painful, destructive emotional illness; both she and her father were set free from drinking. This all occurred because Jesus dug up an emotional trauma which had plagued her from childhood. That is reconciliation!

There are times when emotional suffering deteriorates into mental illnesses. The mind then becomes tormented by the runaway emotions. This can be caused by a number of circumstances: disappointments, bad childhood memories, and too many demands by parents.

Often, psychiatrists (particularly Spirit-filled psychiatrists) can help people. I have worked with them to try to help certain people. But remember, God is the Master Psychiatrist. He created the psyche in each person. Therefore, He knows better than anyone how to heal our minds.

The Holy Spirit can take you right back to the time and place where the initial seeds for mental illness were sown. Why? Because He was right there with you. You may not have been aware of His presence, but He was there.

Often as we minister healing to mentally disturbed people, their faces will light up and they will say, "Oh, Jesus is speaking to me!"

As they walk back through their memories with Jesus, they find themselves in a supernatural state in which Jesus does speak to them. All of this is possible through the reconciliation Jesus provided for us.

Now let's look at the relation between reconciliation and physical healing. The need for physical healing results from disease that is in the world due to original sin and the Fall of Man. Prior to that time, there was no such thing as sickness.

One cause of physical illness is disobedience to God. The apostle Paul emphasized the relationship of sickness to disobedience when he wrote to the Corinthians:

> *Therefore, whoever eats the bread or drinks the cup of the Lord in an unworthy manner will be guilty of sinning against the body and blood of the Lord. A man ought to examine himself before he eats of the bread and drinks of the cup. For anyone who eats and drinks without recognizing the body of the Lord eats and drinks judgment on himself. That is why many among you are weak and sick, and a number of you have fallen asleep* (1 Corinthians 11:27-30).

Unworthy simply means "unconfessed sin" in a person's life. Thus, disobedience to God, when allowed to continue unconfessed, can lead to sickness, which can lead to death—even among Christians.

Another cause of physical illness is the neglect of the body. The Old Testament is filled with teachings on the laws, which apply to good health. There are 436 such commands, which are found primarily in the Books of Leviticus and Deuteronomy.

The New Testament also makes a clear statement addressing how a person ought to care for the physical body. It says, *"Don't you know that you yourselves are God's temple and that God's Spirit lives in you? If anyone destroys God's temple, God will destroy him; for God's temple is sacred, and you are that temple"* (1 Cor. 3:16-17).

There is a distinct relationship between the neglect of the body and illness.

One of the worst body abuses is overeating, which leads to being overweight. As Bill and I travel in the ministry, we often encounter people so large they can hardly walk. Some of them have leg problems, back problems, stomach disorders, heart ailments, and high blood pressure. It is obvious that they are abusing their bodies with the excessive weight they carry around.

Occasionally one of these dear people will say to me, "Pray for God to take this weight off me."

We have seen that happen when God would heal an emotional or physical disorder which caused the problem of obesity. But ordinarily I tell the person, "I'm sorry, most of the time God doesn't do it that way." God wants us to be disciplined, for our own good.

We have seen people with weight problems develop emotional illness. When such illness exists, it is necessary to ferret out the root cause.

Is it fear, doubt, anxiety, poor self-image, insecurity, or what? God often reveals the root cause and the healing process begins.

Reconciliation and God's Healing Ways

All healings are different.

There are times when people are healed instantly. The healing is immediate as everything falls into proper place. In my case, I was so near death, that if I were to survive, God had to restore me immediately.

Most healings take time; but many people don't realize this. I've told people who have come to me for prayer that their healing may take some time. Often one of them will say, "I don't want to be healed that way. I want to be healed right now."

My reply is, "You may not be healed at all if you aren't willing to take it the way the Lord gives it."

Searching the Word builds your faith. Paul told the Romans, *"So then faith cometh by hearing, and hearing by the word of God"* (Rom. 10:17 KJV). As we study the Word, our faith increases and better prepares us to receive healing.

Get serious with God about sin in your life. That sin could be standing in the way of your being healed. *Confess your faults one to another,* as James admonishes us, so that you can be healed (see James 5:16).

If you have bad habits in your life such as smoking, drinking, or overeating, ask God to help you yield those habits to Him. Pray that they be removed from your life. God will do it.

An unforgiving spirit can close us off to a healing. If we refuse to forgive someone, we cut ourselves off from the power of God. That works against reconciliation.

When you have prayed to be healed, be sure to keep a good balance as you claim the healing. There is balance between the positive confession, "I am healed," and the confession, "God is healing me."

I prefer the latter. Why? It seems counterproductive to say a headache is healed when your head is still splitting wide open; or to say that you are healed of arthritis when you can't open your hand or move your fingers. The same is true when you say that you are delivered from smoking, yet you have a cigarette between your fingers, and lungs that are filled with tar and nicotine.

Is it not much wiser to say, "God is healing me" or "I am being healed"? That is far better, since many healings are progressive.

Jesus' ministry included different kinds of healings; some were instantaneous; others were progressive. For instance, when Jesus was in Bethsaida, some people brought a blind man to Him and asked Him to touch the man. Jesus took the blind man by the hand and led him out of the town, where He applied spit to the man's eyes. Then Jesus asked the man if he could see. The man looked up and said he could see men walking, but they looked like trees. At that point, Jesus again put His hands on the man's eyes. Immediately, the man's eyes were completely restored. (See Mark 8:22-26.)

When Jesus first touched him, the blind man could have shouted the positive confession, "I'm healed! I'm healed!" But he wasn't.

He was in the process of being healed. Actually, the blind man's first response was not positive at all. He said, "I see men as trees, walking." He could have run off confessing, "I'm healed," and never have been able to see men as anything but trees. However, he waited on Jesus to complete the healing and was made completely whole.

I have seen people still in pitiful conditions say, "Well, according to the Word of God, I'm healed." But in their hearts they really didn't believe it because they still had the illness in their bodies.

That tends to make people play games with God. So I say, "I still have the physical manifestation of that sickness, but God is healing me. He's bringing me into wholeness."

Believe God is healing your body from the very minute you ask for it, but be sure you have removed all the roadblocks to reconciliation that might hinder the healing.

When you still have every symptom of your sickness, it is so much more exciting to say, "He is healing me," than to say, "I am healed." Every day you will notice a little more healing in your body until you are completely well.

Jesus Himself said, *"Therefore I tell you, whatever you ask for in prayer, believe that you have received it, and it will be yours"* (Mark 11:24).

Note that Jesus did not say, "You already have it." Instead, He said, *"It will be yours."* Remember, God wants you to walk in good health and Jesus is the source of that health.

Confess your inability to heal yourself. That really gets God's attention and makes the devil plenty mad. Say, "I can't do a thing, Lord, so I am totally depending on You. You're the source of my healing; You are all I have."

Another benefit of our reconciliation is that we can ask God to show us the source of our illness. He often shows me the cause of another person's illness. When He reveals the source of an illness, we can follow what He tells us to do—and healing will result.

His Will Be Done

There have been times when God would not allow me to pray for healing. When my father became ill, I went to see him. I wanted to pray for my father to be healed. A prayer was already going through my mind, something like, "Lord, just let him be with us a few more years," or "Maybe, Lord, even for a season, but heal him and let him be with us a while longer."

But the very minute I entered his room and walked over to his bed, the Lord said, "Don't say those words."

I began to pray and these words came out of my mouth: *"Let not your heart be troubled: ye believe in God, believe also in Me"* (John 14:1 KJV). Then I couldn't go on; I couldn't remember the rest of the words, even though I had taught from that Scripture passage many times.

Suddenly, as we left the hospital room to go home, the rest of the passage flooded through my mind:

In My Father's house are many mansions: if it were not so, I would have told you. I go to prepare a place for you. And if I go and prepare a place for you, I will come again, and receive you unto Myself; that where I am, there ye may be also (John 14:2-3 KJV).

After we arrived at home, my mother mentioned that I had not prayed for my father to be healed. "You couldn't pray for him to be healed, could you?" she asked.

"No," I replied.

"Then he is going home and I must release him to the Lord," she said. Later that evening as we prayed together, Mother said, "Lord, I don't want to give him up, but I know You're calling him back to You.

He has always belonged to You anyway. But I just ask that You take him quickly and with no pain."

The next day my father asked for the family lawyer so that he could take care of some last-minute business. The doctor told us he might not be alert enough to talk to his lawyer.

But the following day the lawyer came and my father put everything in order. He had lived a full life and knew he was going home. He died a short time later, quickly and without pain, just as Mother had prayed.

After he died I said, "Mom, isn't it beautiful? Now his body is no longer tired. There's no more sickness, and Dad is seeing all the splendor of God in Heaven."

That is the ultimate healing!

Chapter 12

Walking in Victory

This is the victory that has overcome the world,
even our faith. Who is it that overcomes the world?
Only he who believes that Jesus is the Son of God
(1 John 5:4-5).

The Lord has taught me how to stay free! Every night before I go to bed, I ask Jesus to show me my sin of that day, to show me any feelings that have come into my heart that should not be there. It's amazing what the Lord shows me.

When I first began this practice, I found myself arguing with the Lord. "But that was such a little thing, Lord," I would say after He revealed some sin to me. It's those little sins that pile up and make big sins. Now when the Lord shows me a so-called "little sin," I look at it and say, "All right, Lord, I'm laying it at the foot of the Cross and asking You to heal it right now."

If you will do this daily, before you go to bed, you'll sleep a lot better at night and wake up the next morning feeling good. But if you allow the sins to build up, you must go through some inner emotional cleansing to get rid of them. Remember, it's far easier to stay free than to have to be set free.

Walking in victory has so many wonderful by-products. The Lord proves His love for us through good things. For instance, you will recall that during the final stages of my terminal illness, I often overcame the excruciating pain by imagining that I was on a mountain looking down at a little river in the valley below.

I could almost smell the wildflowers and taste the clean air right there in my bed. Well, God later took me to the exact place which, during my illness, had brought me much-needed relief from pain.

A minister and his wife, our close friends, owned a cabin in the mountains of New Mexico. They invited me to go with them to the cabin for a few days of rest from the long days and nights of ministry. Bill had to work and couldn't go, but he urged me to join them; so I went with them.

When we arrived on top of the mountain, it suddenly hit me: that was the exact spot God allowed me to see during my illness! The wildflowers and the little ribbon of a river down below were exactly as God had shown me earlier. Even the rocks were the same.

Healing and the Church

Sometimes the Holy Spirit shows me the chains, the bonds satan uses to keep people from victory. So many of God's people say: "I was healed, but God took it away," or "I was healed, but I lost my healing." That's not true! God would never take away a gift He has given to one of His children.

The truth is, people refuse to walk in victory and satan brings illness back into their lives. Often, they don't even know how to carry on spiritual warfare in order to guard against it. Walking in victory requires putting our lives in order and establishing the proper priorities.

First, we must have Jesus as our Savior and Healer. Then, we must accept the fullness that He brings us through the Holy Spirit. When we believe and receive the baptism in the Holy Spirit, we experience that wonderful infilling. Without it, we can receive very little from the Lord.

Healing belongs in the churches. Deliverance belongs in the churches. If this were a reality, we would not see all the extravagances that exist in healing ministries today.

I learned very quickly what God meant when He told me to "Keep the balance and educate My people." God has given me a vision to see our churches so open to the Holy Spirit that, on Sunday mornings, the ministers will say, "Are there any sick among you? Come to the altar now—it's time for prayer for the sick." Then, people in the congregation will anoint the sick with oil, pray for them, and they will be healed. One day we will see this happen in our churches.

Praise God for local churches where people are healed. May they increase!

Learning Whether to Receive or Reject

Isn't it scary that we Christians have such misconceptions of the Holy Spirit? He wants to heal us and keep us living in abundant health, but so many of us still know so little about Him and His work.

Here is how I'm learning to know Jesus (and it is so beautiful): I carefully search the Scriptures and read all about Him. Then I pray, "All right, Lord, put me right there with You."

One day I was praying on the phone with a woman from Florida. As we prayed about some problems she was encountering, I suddenly told her, "You must go to the Garden of Gethsemane with Jesus. You have to be right there with Him as the soldiers take Him away. You have to be with Him in the courtyard where He is being whipped. Walk with Him all the way to Calvary."

As we prayed, I took her through Jesus' steps from the garden, with all the agony He went through and the agony we must go through to know Him. It is important for us to be there with Him while they beat Him, cut His back to shreds, and press the crown of thorns onto His head so hard that the blood flowed like a river.

After a pause, I asked the woman on the phone, "Do you see how the cobblestones cut His feet to ribbons?" In the Spirit, I could see that the cobblestones had sharp, jagged points which cut His feet because His shoes had been taken away, leaving Him barefoot. I saw His footprints of blood along the cobblestone road.

"That's how you learn Jesus," I told the woman.

That simple exercise of being with Jesus helped the woman so much that her problems just seemed to fade away. That's walking in victory!

Jesus once told His detractors, *"...Ye do err, not knowing the scriptures, nor the power of God"* (Matt. 22:29 KJV). That speaks so clearly to all of us today. We know the words in our Bible, but not what they mean. How can we know unless we have the fullness of the Spirit to bring forth the truth of the Word?

Our Lord also said, "I'll not leave you alone. I will send you another Comforter. And when He comes you will know the truth. He will teach you the truth." (See John 14:16-18, 26; 15:26; 16:13.)

We're beginning to know and understand the truth of our God. In that understanding we find there is healing for the body, mind, and spirit.

Some time ago, we closed out a three-week teaching seminar on healing. On the last night of the seminar, I invited each person there to trade in the ashes of their lives for the beauty of Jesus. When we learn to do that, we walk in victory.

God is calling His people to be strong. He is through coddling us. There will be bad days ahead. The weak will fall by the wayside. Only the strong—those walking in victory—will stand.

From a physical standpoint, walking in victory means being unwilling to accept sickness. I accepted my illness probably because my grandfather died with a deteriorated spine and cancer the year before I became ill. I accepted the spine disease but kept telling myself, "I'll not die as Pap did with cancer."

After my healing, one doctor said, "You know, Delores, we've never understood why you didn't have cancer. Your bones and every organ of your body were ripe for cancer."

Then the Lord brought me to the understanding of why I didn't get cancer—I wouldn't accept it. I was dying in far worse condition than my grandfather died, but I never accepted the cancer. Every time cancer crossed my mind, I rejected it, without really knowing what I was doing.

We must learn to reject what the enemy tries to put on us, for he is the one who brings sickness. I held out my hands to the evil one and received the spine disease, the herniated esophagus, the heart, kidney, and bowel conditions, and all the rest—but I did not receive cancer. If you resist illness by refusing it, satan has a hard time laying it on you!

If we are to walk in victory, we also must guard our relationships. God will help us set our relationships in their proper order: primary is our relationship to Him; next, is our relationship with family; third, is our relationship to authority; and finally, we have relationships with the people we meet at the supermarket or on the street.

I've discovered that the check-out counter at the supermarket is a place that creates an opportunity to show a clerk the love of Jesus. Yet, what do most people do? They get angry because the line is so long and the clerk is slow.

We have days when our attitudes just go crazy because we are human. The old nature always works at getting the upper hand, and when our attitudes go bad, they usually affect the ones we love. When you allow a bad attitude to continue, your body starts to feel the wear and tear of it. It affects your mind and emotions; before long, you are sick. All because of a bad attitude.

Unfortunately, our bad attitudes sometimes cause us to take out our anger, frustrations, and disappointments on our children. Who can you pick on who can't fight back? Your children.

You can get so frustrated, you feel like lashing out at your husband. But you dare not. Instead, your child is sitting there, minding his own business, and you blast him—an innocent bystander.

A husband acts the same way when his attitude goes bad. For instance, he may have a problem at work; his relationships with co-workers may be making him uptight all the time. Yet he must smile and be courteous to them, regardless of how he really feels. Filled with pent-up anger, he may feel like lashing out against his family. Wives and children take a lot of abuse because husbands get uptight at work and come home with bad attitudes.

God gave you those children to raise in love. He placed them in your arms so they would feel secure. Instead, when you take out your frustrations on them, they tend to grow up feeling insecure. Because of what they learn in the home they become prone to taking out their frustrations on their own children. Thus, a vicious cycle is perpetuated.

Insecurity among children often leads to all kinds of disciplinary problems. These problems develop incrementally until one day you find yourself saying, "I don't know why this child turned out the way he did."

Taking out your bad attitude on your children is a sure sign you are not walking in victory. It is easy to overcome such an attitude. The very minute your attitude starts to turn sour, begin praising the Lord for something good that is happening in your life. Savor the presence of the Holy Spirit. Rebuke the attitude in the name of Jesus. Take authority over it. If you've wronged a family member, ask for forgiveness.

Spiritual sickness that results from personal sin is another barrier to walking in victory. I know people who once walked in victory, yet personal sin led them away from the Lord.

Often those in ministry are afraid to share with anyone else the doubts, fears, and relational struggles they experience. However, the Bible never tries to hide a thing. Even the patriarchs and saints are portrayed as they really were, men and women with feet of clay, subject to every temptation. If you find that hard to believe, read again the stories of Adam, Abraham, Sarah, Noah, David, Solomon, Simon Peter, and John Mark.

People around us are not fooled. They know when we are faking it and failing to be open and honest with them.

Children of God who want to walk in victory must accept the gifts of the Holy Spirit that are available to them. Many never do that. For instance, I'm confident there are thousands of people who receive the gift of knowledge yet are afraid to exercise it.

During a prayer time or a worship service, God may reveal that He is healing someone who is there. The person who receives the word of knowledge must call out the healing or satan may try to snatch it away before the one who is being healed has the opportunity to receive it.

Some people are lazy and that causes them to be hesitant about ministering the gifts. Then there is fear of peer pressure. People often don't want to be accused of being too religious. Satan uses peer pressure, even in the family. A woman may ask, "What will my husband think if I start calling out healings?"

Walking in the Spirit

Walking in victory is synonymous with walking in the Spirit. It is easy to be filled with the Spirit, but it's quite another matter to walk in the Spirit, which is much more important. And people often confuse the two concepts.

Immediately after receiving the baptism, a person should begin to devour the Word of God. Do a word study on the Holy Spirit. Find out everything you can about His work in your life. Then you will understand better what He does, how He operates, and what His ministry is. Any Bible concordance will give you all the biblical references related to Him. You will learn: who He is, when He came, how He worked through the Old Testament prophets, and how He came to Jesus. You will also come to understand His availability, the nature of His influence on the Church, and the ways in which He works today.

After your word study on the Holy Spirit, do a word study on Jesus. As you study the ministry of Jesus, you will become acquainted with salvation, healing, deliverance from unclean spirits, and the inner healing of the brokenhearted. You will also learn how He dealt with people such as the woman at the well (see John 4). Deep within, she had a broken heart. That's why she committed adultery with so many men. Jesus healed her and she became a strong witness for Him.

The Holy Spirit continues the ministry of Jesus today through His people. Therefore, in order to understand the work of the Holy Spirit, it is important for us to become intimate with Jesus. Many people receive the baptism in the Holy Spirit, yet they never understand the implications because they are not intimate with Jesus. They just go off on a fling. It makes a bad impression and turns other people away from the baptism. They get a prayer language and immediately start trying to push it off on everyone they meet. God brings people into the baptism in His own good timing. Don't push it down people's throats; it doesn't work that way.

When we receive the baptism in the Holy Spirit, then we must serve the Lord by serving people. It's not just a great big glory time! I see a lot of people using the baptism only for glory time, but then what happens? They leak. David said, *"...my cup runneth over"* (Ps. 23:5 KJV). But some of our cups have holes in them.

D.L. Moody was once asked why he repeatedly sought the infilling of the Holy Spirit. "Because I leak a lot," he replied.

We are like spiritual sieves. We're human. We leak. We must be refilled. People don't realize this. They run from miracle service to miracle service. They get excited when the blind see, when the lame walk, and when people are delivered from unclean spirits. But many of those people won't go across the street to witness to a neighbor about Christ, or pray for a sick child, or sit still for a teaching! Then one day a person like that finds himself at home alone; suddenly all the excitement is gone and discouragement sets in.

Why? Because they are not established in the Word. They don't really understand Jesus and the Holy Spirit. They have no intimate relationship with them.

Each of us is subject to discouragement and most of the time it hits us when we are alone. I get discouraged at times and just want to run home and shut the door. But then I realize that Jesus is right there with me; that makes me feel good. Just to know that I can talk to Him and tell Him exactly what is on my heart—knowing He will understand and give me peace and love—that's walking in victory!

Then, there are people who want the gifts of the Spirit, but not the fruit of the Spirit. If we don't want to develop the fruit, then forget the gifts. I have seen people who received the gifts before they learned about the fruit. That is sad. They won't last. Why? Because the fruit of the Spirit are characteristic of Jesus.

Remember, if you are established in the Word, you can get just as excited over the presence of the Lord while driving down the highway in your automobile as in some great miracle service.

Let me share a little secret: I hate a messy house.

Our Chris was working on a job where he got really dirty. After he took a bath, the tub was always black. Although we encouraged him to clean the tub, like most boys, he seldom remembered. It was usually left for Mama to clean. Does that sound familiar?

I would look at that dirty, black bathtub, and it would gripe me. Then I would get angry and think, "Why should I clean his dirty tub? He doesn't appreciate anything I do. What's the matter with that boy? No one appreciates me."

Thankfully, I learned that when things like that happen, I could start praising the Lord. I realized that, instead of getting myself in an uproar. I could begin to say, "Thank You, Jesus, that Chris is healthy. Thank You, Jesus, that he's not off somewhere on drugs." You know what? When I did that, it was easy to clean that black, dirty bathtub.

The secret is in praising God rather than only looking at the job before us. But that was something God had to teach me. There were times when I griped and remained irritated for hours over the bathtub.

Satan is crafty and uses situations in the home to drive a wedge between loved ones. Remember, satan attacks your mind. If your mind is centered on Jesus, you can ward off the attack.

People are so fearful today; satan has them all bound up in fear. And fear keeps many people from receiving the fullness of the Holy Spirit. When we keep our minds on Jesus, we are free from fear.

Satan will twist and turn God's Word so people can't see things as they really are in the Scriptures. Each morning a Christian should pray, "Lord, reveal what You have for me today," and then accept what God reveals. Fear leaves when we walk in God's revelation.

Too many people are running around bringing others into the baptism of the Holy Spirit, never taking the time to establish them in the faith and never helping them learn to walk in the Spirit.

We Christians try to complicate everything. Oh, if we would only be satisfied with the straightforward ways Jesus wants to teach us! It is so simple. When we wake up in the morning we can say, "Good morning, Lord. Give me the strength and wisdom to do what You would have me do today." That's my first prayer every morning.

If everyone who has come into the baptism and the fullness of the Spirit would start their day with a prayer like that, so many people would get turned on to Jesus. Instead, many are discontented and say, "Oh, I have to stay home all day. I have kids to take care of, you know." God can be just as real to a mother at home taking care of her children as to the evangelist out in the great miracle service.

Remember, Peter preached at Pentecost and 3,000 were saved, but he spent most of his time teaching in little churches, helping Christians grow. Paul was much the same. He talked about the patience necessary to help new Christians grow up. I love to teach individuals and small groups.

All the glory time is great—in its proper place, but it's only the tip of the iceberg. The essential element in the Christian faith is growth.

Victory in Witnessing

Walking in victory also means witnessing to our faith. We're not to force Jesus on anyone; that doesn't work. Jesus never forced Himself on anyone. There will come a time when you are having a cup of coffee with a neighbor who has a headache, or a sore arm, leg, or back. You can say, "You know, I believe Jesus is our Healer. I would like to pray for you that He would take this pain away and heal you."

It is just that simple. You can bring someone to Jesus through prayer for a headache. Just pray and leave it alone. Unless something drastic is causing the illness, God will heal it immediately, as a witness.

In the next day or two that person will see you and say, "Hey, you know when you prayed for me, my headache disappeared."

You can reply casually, "Yes, I know. The Lord does that. We pray for things like that all the time."

Thus you have opened a door through which Jesus can walk into that person's life. Then you can open the Bible and show the person how to be saved and filled with the Holy Spirit.

You walk in victory as you guard your mind. The Lord renews your mind as you keep it fixed on Him. He continues to forgive your sins, and wash you white as snow. He covers all your guilt in His blood and remembers your sin no more.

That's walking in victory!

The Winders' Ministry

Delores and Bill Winder are humble, obedient servants of the Lord. Their ministry call is primarily to the denominational church. Their goal is to fulfill the Great Commission, making disciples according to Jesus' command.

The hallmark of their ministry is to continually point people to Jesus as the One who meets their needs. As the Lord heals people in their meetings, the Winders ask the people to turn and pray for healing for others.

Bill and Delores have always stressed that a Christian's walk is a relationship with the living Lord. Simply observing them in ministry and seeing the fruit borne through them by the Holy Spirit is ample evidence of their living out of that relationship. Their obedience to the Lord Jesus Christ continues to be a powerful witness to many.

The following prayers are offered by Delores to assist anyone desiring either to come into fellowship with Jesus, or to surrender more fully to Him.

Prayer for Salvation

Jesus, I ask You to come into my life. I confess that I am a sinner and cannot save myself. You are the Son of God who came to forgive me of my sins and to give me eternal life. I accept Your sacrifice for me on the Cross and Your resurrection from the grave. Thank You for Your love for me. I give You my life to control for the rest of my days. I commit my life to You. (Read Isaiah 1:18 and John 3:16.)

Prayer for the Baptism of the Holy Spirit

Jesus will baptize you with the Holy Spirit and fire (see Matt. 3:11). The Holy Spirit comes when we accept Jesus as Savior; but we need to ask to be filled and empowered by Him. He is called our Helper, the Spirit of Truth who teaches us all truth.

Lord Jesus, fill me with the Holy Spirit. I give Him control of my life. Empower me to be Your witness and to do the work of a disciple. Holy Spirit, let Your gifts flow through me and help me bear much fruit to further the Kingdom of God. Thank You, Lord Jesus.

References:

John 15:26-27—Helper (Comforter), Spirit of Truth

Acts 1:8—Power to witness

Galatians 5:22-23—Fruit of the Spirit

Romans 12:6-8; 1 Corinthians 12:7-10—Gifts of the Spirit

Pictured left to right: Jean Hunter, Nashville, TN: Tumors in head, four years of illness, nothing more could be done. Healed instantly on February 11, 1987! Steve Bramham, Kinnesaw, GA: Severe back problems for 14 years, surgeries, constant pain. Given his wheelchair at V.A. the day before his healing; nothing more could be done. Healed instantly on June 5, 1999! Betty Rambin, Shreveport, LA: Three types of non-treatable cancer. Nurse, wife of retired Southern Baptist pastor. Victoriously healed!

God healed this young man, crippled since he was five years old, during a Winder ministry trip in New Zealand.

Standing to my left, Reverend and Mrs. Norman Dyer, who were there the night I was healed. Great friends! They followed our ministry and stood in awe at the Holy Spirit's work. Norman is now with the Lord (Photo taken in 1988).

Andrea, Amanda, Bridget, and Chris Winder.

Delores encourages believers to pray for each other and receives "words of knowledge" about people's prayer needs.

Fellowship Foundation, Inc.
Bill & Delores Winder Ministry
P.O. Box 19370
Shreveport, LA 71149-0370

APPENDIX

[The following is the 10th chapter of *Real Miracles*, a book by H. Richard Casdorph, M.D., Ph.D., F.A.C.P. It is reprinted with the kind permission of Bridge-Logos, Orlando, Florida USA (1-800-631-5802).]

Osteoporosis of the Entire Spine With Intractable Pain Requiring Bilateral Cordotomies
Delores Winder

D elores Winder was a devout Presbyterian and it was with great reluctance that she contemplated attending a Methodist convention on the Holy Spirit scheduled for August 30, 1975.

Kathryn Kuhlman, whom she had never watched on television because she didn't believe in that kind of healing, was going to be speaking. But a friend questioned her, "What if you're keeping a door closed?" It was only then that she prayed about it and decided she should go.

Miss Kuhlman spoke of the Holy Spirit's presence and ability to do anything. Then she prayed and Delores realized that her legs were on fire. The sensation startled her because her bilateral cordotomies, which had been done to relieve severe pain in her spine and lower extremities,

171

had left her without any feeling in her legs. But she put it out of her mind.

When Miss Kuhlman prayed with someone up on the stage and the person fell to the floor, Delores' misgivings were confirmed. The service had been so beautiful, why, she wondered, did Miss Kuhlman have to spoil it with such theatrical demonstrations. She turned to her friend, "Let's go." Before her friend could answer, a stranger asked Delores why she wore a neck brace. "I have a bad neck."

"Something is happening, isn't it?"

"Well, my legs are burning like crazy."

"Do you want to talk more about it?"

"Yes, outside."

So he helped Delores up and they started out of the building. He asked about her surgeries and she mentioned casually that she had had four spinal fusions and two cordotomies. She expected him to ask her what a cordotomy was. Instead he remarked, "And your legs are burning. Isn't that strange?"

When they got to the rear of the auditorium he told Delores she could take off her cast if she wanted to. Delores had worn a body cast for fourteen years. She started to object but she had a feeling he knew something she didn't. She accepted his advice and he escorted her back into the auditorium whereupon Miss Kuhlman asked them to come up on the stage. It was then that she learned who this mysterious stranger was: Dr. Richard Owellen of Johns Hopkins Medical School, a loyal friend and supporter of Miss Kuhlman.

I will let Delores take up the story at this point:

At no time did I believe this was possible. Yet I had no pain. I was walking without my cast. I'd even gotten rid of my headache and I could feel my legs. It was utterly fantastic to me. My mind was reeling and I was not certain of anything. My son had said before I left that I would be healed. But I had ruled out even the possibility of such a thing.

When Miss Kuhlman touched me I was sure I would not go down, but I did. Two weeks later in Oklahoma City she touched me again and I felt as if plugs were pulled from the bottom of my feet and everything drained out of me. It was like being wrapped in the arms of a great love. My husband and son were aware of this too. On the way home, unintelligible words were running through my mind. When I picked up my Bible after this it was like I had never read it before. I began to know things I had no way of knowing. I got feelings about people or something I ought to do that made no sense, yet, when I did what those feelings suggested, I soon discovered the reason.

I am now speaking regularly in churches and never know what I'm going to say—I just pray. He speaks the words and, so far, it has gone well. I still do not like the publicity, but a wise person told me, "You're the package God put a miracle in and people need to see the package."

Delores Winder holding the cast she had
worn for the last eighteen months prior
to her healing. She had worn out seven
casts in the preceding fourteen years. In
her right hand is her neck brace.

Mrs. Winder's medical history in her own testimony follows:

*Between January 1957, and August 1972, I had four back fusions
(lower lumbar), another operation to remove spurs from the fusion, and two
cordotomies. The first fusion was done to correct three deformed vertebrae
and scoliosis. It held three years, and then broke. I returned to the same surgeon and had the second fusion. It was not long before I had further trouble. In 1964 I had to have spikes removed. Then I spent much time in bed*

and in a plaster-of-Paris cast. My family doctor was giving me novocaine injections in the spine along with pain medication. In 1966 I was hospitalized. After x-rays and consultation with an internal medicine specialist they diagnosed my problem as pseudoarthrosis and osteoporosis.

The doctor decided to do a frontal fusion (a frontal fusion approaches the spinal column from the front through the abdomen rather than from the back) hoping there would be less pressure and it would hold. It held about eighteen months. Then they did the first percutaneous cordotomy. This was on the right side and was done to the neck level. After a time the fusion broke again and they did the fourth fusion.

Then, in 1972, I had the second cordotomy (for the opposite side of the body). This one could only be taken to a little above waist level because my lungs were not strong enough to take it higher. I still had intense pain above that level and, in 1973, I fell. That started the trouble in my neck and left shoulder and I had to go into a Queen Anne collar. I had very bad headaches and could not turn my head. My shoulder hurt so much that when the doctor examined me, he could not put much pressure on it until after my healing.

I was on pain medication, tranquilizers and at least six other medications all the time. There were complications too. I was also taking medicines for kidney, stomach, low blood pressure, and bowel conditions. In addition, I had a herniated esophagus. After my fall in 1973, they could not stabilize my general health.

In January 1975, the neurosurgeon did another myelogram and told me nothing more could be done, but that I would live longer by going to bed and staying still. Before this I was only allowed out of bed three hours a day, one hour at a time. After much prayer, my husband and I decided I should continue to be up as much as I could manage. I was getting weaker all the time, but did not want my fourteen-year-old son to remember me in a hospital bed.

Medical Documentation

I have medical records on this lady over an inch thick. They document her story and I will only briefly summarize them here. Cordotomies are normally reserved for patients with cancer and extreme pain. This alone should illustrate that she does not exaggerate the severity of her condition.

In summary:

1) Lumbar spine fusion, 1957, with bone grafts from tibia. Spinal fusion of 3rd, 4th and 5th lumbar vertebrae.

2) Repeat spinal fusion with bone graft from tibia, 1961, due to trauma when the patient broke the first graft.

3) In 1965 the patient had excision of spinous processes thought to be contributing to pain. The graft was reported to be solid at this time.

4) In 1967 the patient had anterior interbody fusion, L-3-4, L-4-5, L-5-S-1.

5) In 1968 a percutaneous cordotomy was performed after severe pain had continued. This was done in Dallas, Texas, at Parkland Memorial Hospital for relief of right side pain. The physicians regarded it as very successful.

6) In 1970 the patient underwent her fourth fusion of the lumbar spine because of recurrence of pain. Patient continued to have pain. She was fitted with two molded plastic body casts and took several Talwin tablets per day and occasionally had injections of Talwin for relief of pain.

7) August, 1972, the patient underwent a second percutaneous cordotomy down at level C-6 and C-7 with good relief of her

pain. This was done to relieve the pain on the left side of the body and removed all sensation on the left up to the waist level. This was done at Fort Worth, Texas.

Unfortunately, the patient had recurrent pain in other parts of her body even after the cordotomies and she was left with altered and decreased sensation in the lower extremities. She had a gradual downhill course, as described in her testimony, up to the time of her healing. Since that time she has been leading a completely normal life without medication, braces or body cast. The medical diagnoses in this case include:

1) Extensive osteoporosis of the spine.

2) Pseudoarthrosis of the spine.

3) Severe intractable pain requiring bilateral percutaneous cordotomy for relief.

4) Status post-operative laminectomy and fusion x4.

5) Trauma to the right shoulder and neck with pain.

The medical records indicate that in spite of bilateral cordotomies, an extreme procedure, the patient gradually had a recurrence of pain in the low back, neck and shoulders requiring injections for local relief of pain. The records indicate that this discomfort was becoming progressively worse and that it was unrelated to trauma or overactivity.

According to medical records dated May 22, 1974, she was taking Percodan, or Phenergan, and Talwin. She was losing weight, getting around poorly, and had to be helped on and off the table. There were restricted movements of her lower back with localized discomfort.

The last note in the medical records before her healing is dated August 6, 1975. Her physician remarked that she did not look good; she felt poorly, was depressed with back discomfort at the level of D-6-7.

Her nails were cracking and she also had an ulcerated area about her lower back where the brace irritated the skin.

The last notation on her chart was made, after her healing, on September 3, 1975. The physician commented that the patient had had some sort of "faith healing" experience and had apparently "gotten an excellent result physically and…emotionally.…Her girdle…does not fit her because she stands up so much straighter." He thought the feeling in her feet wasn't quite normal, but that her back was more mobile, her neck and shoulders better, and her leg signs negative.

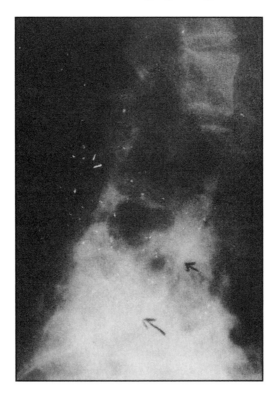

This x-ray of Delores Winder's lumbar spine was obtained January 15, 1975. The radiologist interpreted it to show

> moderate osteoporosis (that is, thinning of the amount of calcium and protein in the bones). The arrows in the front or anterior part of the lumbar spine show disc disease and the sites of the anterior interbody fusion, that is, the fusion of the anterior or front part of the lumbar spine.

Mrs. Winder acknowledged that following her healing on August 30, 1975, she did have a slight residual numbness in the front part of the hip areas and burning in the posterior hip areas. However, after Miss Kuhlman prayed for her and she fell to the floor, all feeling became normal and she has since been free of pain.

To relieve or at least control the severe and disabling pain which this patient experienced over a period of many years, physicians elected to employ a surgical oblative technique known as percutaneous cordotomy. Since this is an unusual technique of which the reader may not be aware, a short discussion of cordotomy follows.

Spinal Cordotomy for Relief of Intractable and Disabling Pain

Spinal cordotomy (literally, cutting the spinal cord) is particularly useful for the relief of widespread pain in the trunk and extremities. It is especially helpful when the pain originates from the thoracic or abdominal regions. Surgeons cut the cord opposite the side of the pain in the anterolateral quadrant of the spinal cord at least six cord segments above the origin of the pain.

The analgesia (relief of pain) resulting from a cordotomy covers the opposite half of the body beginning several segments below the point at which the cord is cut. For complete relief of pain the entire lateral spinothalmic tract must be cut through. Anything less might allow pain to persist. Delores Winder underwent percutaneous cervical cordotomy. This means that, instead of opening her surgically, the doctors inserted a needle through the skin into the spinal cord in order to interrupt the spinothalmic pathways. This technique was introduced by Mullan in 1963 and has proven useful in patients who could not withstand the rigors of conventional surgery on the spinal cord.

Since this technique does not permit the surgeon to see what he is doing, x-ray is used to guide a coagulating needle into the anterolateral quadrant of the spinal cord, usually between the first and second cervical vertebrae. Electrical stimulation can be used to test the location of the needle tip within the spinal cord.

The lateral spinothalamic tract can be coagulated by means of a high frequency electrical current. It remains, however, a blind operation and the surgeon must exercise care not to misplace the lesion and cause additional neurologic deficit, such as paralysis. One risk of the percutaneous technique is that the high cervical cord lesions may interfere with breathing. A percutaneous cordotomy is most commonly applied to poor risk patients with short life expectancy.

Anatomic Considerations

The cordotomy is based on precise anatomic and physiological knowledge. The fibers which carry pain to the cerebrum enter the spinal cord, ascend a few segments, cross the midline, and form the anterolateral tract. Because about ninety percent of pain fibers cross, a cordotomy performed on one side of the spinal cord relieves pain on the opposite side of the body.

The anterolateral (spinothalamic) tract tends to be segmented with the sacral fibers peripherally near the equator while the thoracic and cervical fibers lie more anteriorly and medially. The dentate ligament, which supports the spinal cord, stands between the motor corticospinal tract posteriorly (behind) and the sensory anterolateral tract anteriorly (in front). Thus, if we know the position of the dentate ligament, we can also ascertain the position of the anterolateral tract.

Technique of Percutaneous Cervical Cordotomy

The patient is sedated and lies face down with his or her head fixed in a suitable holder. A spinal needle is inserted between the first and second cervical vertebra below the mastoid process under local anesthesia and the cerebrospinal fluid obtained. An emulsion of iophendylate is injected. This settles on the dentate ligament, which appears as a line across the x-ray film. The anterior border of the cord is usually apparent too. The spinal needle tip is then aimed two millimeters in front of the dentate ligament by raising the hub with an elevator; in other words it points at the anterolateral tract. The depth of penetration is checked by an anterolateral film.

Stimulation Studies and Coagulation

Following this, stimulation studies are carried out with a suitable electric current. If the electrode is correctly positioned in the anterolateral tract, stimulation will produce parasthesias (pins and needles sensation) on the opposite side of the body, which the patient can report. If the electrode is incorrectly situated in the motor tract, it will cause movement of the body on the same side. If the electrode is situated in the anterior horn cells, then movement of the neck muscles on the same side will occur.

When the electrode is in the correct position, the anterolateral (spinothalamic) tract is coagulated. A radio-frequency current produces a heat lesion. Each lesion generator has to be standardized to produce a lesion of about twenty square millimeters in about thirty seconds.

During and between coagulation, physicians check the patient's motor power. If they detect the slightest suggestion of motor weakness, the procedure is stopped. Also, between coagulations, they check the reduction of pain on the opposite side of the body by pin-prick testing.

In summary, percutaneous cervical cordotomy is a technique applied for pain relief in patients with incapacitating and disabling pain. It is most commonly applied to terminal cancer patients, although occasionally to others, like Delores Winder, who suffer chronic, severe and disabling pain.*

Comments

Mrs. Delores Winder presents us with an unusual case of severe, chronic, disabling pain secondary to osteoporosis, which her physicians tried to relieve by five different spine operations. In desperation they resorted to a bilateral percutaneous cordotomy.

This patient's symptoms had begun early in 1957. After 1962 she had worn a full-body cast or brace of some sort. Most of the time it was a full-body cast, although at the time of her healing she was in a light-weight, full-body plastic shell.

Although she did not believe in instant miraculous healing, she attended a lecture by Miss Kuhlman in Dallas on August 30, 1975. She was miraculously healed beginning with a sensation of heat in both lower extremities from the thighs down.

---

* Dr. Anselmo Pineda, M.D., F.A.C.S., was kind enough to review this chapter with special attention to the section dealing with spinal cordotomy for control of pain. Dr. Pineda is a Diplomate of the American Board of Neurosurgery and is widely regarded as an authority in the field of control of pain problems by the use of various neurosurgical techniques, including the implantation of neuropacemakers.

She has been restored to full health, wears no brace or support, takes no medication, and has completely normal sensations in the lower extremities. This is unusual because the spinothalamic nerve tracts in the spinal cord had been interrupted on both sides and, in such cases, the ensuing numbness is usually permanent.

Delores doesn't enjoy being before the public—as she often has been since her healing—but she obediently proclaims the miracle working power of God as she learns to walk in the Spirit.

HEALINGS I HAVE EXPERIENCED

_____
_____
_____
_____
_____
_____
_____
_____
_____
_____
_____

HEALINGS OTHERS HAVE EXPERIENCED

_____

_____

_____

_____

_____

_____

_____

_____

_____

_____

_____

_____

_____

_____

_____

_____

_____

_____

_____

_____

_____

_____

_____

_____

_____

_____

_____

_____

_____

_____

_____

_____

_____

_____

_____

_____

_____

_____

_____

_____

_____

_____

_____

_____

_____

_____

_____

_____

_____

_____

_____

_____

_____

_____

_____